D1577939

Exotic Animal Formulary

Second Edition

Natalie Antinoff, DVM, Diplomate ABVP (Avian Practice)
Thomas H. Boyer, DVM
Susan A. Brown, DVM
John E. Harkness, DVM, MS, MEd
Peter S. Sakas, DVM, MS

Exotic Animal Formulary
Second Edition

Many thanks to the AAHA Press Editorial Advisory Board:
Dr. Laurel Collins, ABVP
Dr. Richard Goebel
Dr. Charles Hickey
Dr. Clayton McKinnon
Dr. Richard Nelson, ABVP
Dr. Hal Taylor

AAHA Press
12575 W. Bayaud Avenue
Lakewood, Colorado 80228

©1999 by AAHA Press

All rights reserved. No part of this publication may be reproduced or transmitted in any form or by any means, electronic or mechanical, including photocopy, recording, or any information storage and retrieval system, without permission in writing from the publisher.

ISBN 1-58326-000-5

Contents

Foreword

The information in this formulary derives from the second editions of the Exotics Series. The titles included in that series are:

Essentials of Rodents: A Guide for Practitioners by John Harkness, DVM, MS, MEd

Essentials of Reptiles: A Guide for Practitioners by Thomas H. Boyer, DVM

Essentials of Ferrets: A Guide for Practitioners by Karen Purcell, DVM

Essentials of Rabbits: A Guide for Practitioners by Natalie Antinoff, DVM, Diplomate ABVP (Avian Practice)

Essentials of Avian Medicine: A Guide for Practitioners by Peter Sakas, DVM, MS

Since the publication of the first edition of this book, veterinary care for exotic pets has become increasingly more common. With this increase has come an increased need by veterinarians to use drugs and dosages to effectively treat these pets. To that end, the authors have created detailed formularies for the species noted. Each section begins with general guidelines that are followed by a table that lists drug dosage and route along with useful comments.

Disclaimer

The Authors and AAHA do not assume responsibility for and make no representation about the suitability or accuracy of the information contained in this work for any purpose, and make no warranties, either express or implied, including the warranties of merchantability and fitness for a particular purpose. Neither AAHA nor the Authors shall be held liable for adverse reactions to or damage resulting from the application of this information including, but not limited to, behavior therapy or drug identification, usage dosage, or equivalency or resulting from any misstatement or error contained in this work. The condition of a specific patient or individual circumstance may warrant alterations in drug dosages or treatments from those set forth. Package information provided by manufacturers should always be reviewed before administration or preparation. Rapid advances in veterinary medicine may cause information contained herein to become outdated, invalid or subject to debate by various veterinary professionals. AAHA and Authors are not to be held responsible for any inaccuracies, omissions or editorial errors, nor for any conse-quences resulting therefrom. AAHA and the Authors shall be held harmless from any and all claims that may arise as a result of any reliance on the information provided.

Avian Drug Dosages
Peter S. Sakas, DVM, MS

General Guidelines

Although avian therapeutics and drug dosages are available from many sources, including scientific articles[1] and formularies in certain avian texts,[2-5] drug dosages in birds are poorly established.[1] Most drugs used in avian medicine have not been tested in pharmacologic studies; rather, the dosages are empirically based or based on clinical experience.

It is important to note that drugs that are effective in certain avian species may be inappropriate or toxic in others.[5] In the critically ill bird, stabilization of the bird is essential. Antibiotic therapy alone is not adequate. Before diagnostic testing or treatments have begun, the practitioner needs to evaluate the hydration status and condition of the bird to determine if fluid therapy and/or nutritional support is needed.[5]

Selection of rational drug therapy is dependent upon several factors, including the condition of the bird, diagnostic findings, culture and sensitivity results, and the capability of the owners to medicate the bird. Although injectable medications are the ideal means of medicating a bird, quite frequently the owners are reluctant to treat the bird in this fashion. Oral administration is the next best technique and the means most often employed in avian practice. Although it takes some time to teach clients how to medicate a bird, once they have become adept at the procedure they can administer an accurate, measured dose. Most medications given in drinking water generally are not as effective as those given by injection or oral treatment. Medication in drinking water loses potency over time. Further, it may discolor the water and cause it to be distasteful, which will lead to nonacceptance by the bird. For birds that are ill and perhaps slightly dehydrated, this situation could lead to further deterioration of their condition. Still another factor is the variable water consumption of birds; one can never be certain that birds are achieving therapeutic levels of drugs that have been administered in their drinking water. Nonetheless, medicated water makes it easy to treat birds on a flock or aviary basis and is often the only means of treating an overtly wild or aggressive bird. If medications are given through the drinking water, bird owners should be instructed to limit foods that have a high water content, such as fruits and vegetables, to prevent the bird's avoidance of the medicated water due to hydration via the food.[5]

Additional Guidelines for Specific Drug Categories

Antimicrobial Agents

Antimicrobials may be the most abused and the most useful class of drugs available to the veterinary practitioner.[5] Bacterial disease is one of the most common medical problems seen in pet birds.[1] Although primary bacterial infections occur, secondary infections due to poor husbandry practices and immunosuppression are more common.[1] Poor husbandry can expose birds to large numbers of potentially pathogenic organisms from environmental sources and other birds.[1] Malnutrition, stress, medications, or concurrent disease may result in immunosuppression with increased susceptibility to potential pathogens.[1] Bacterial disease management in pet birds thus involves determining the causes or sources of the infections, correcting poor husbandry practices, and treating with appropriate antimicrobial therapy.[1]

Bacterial culture and sensitivity are extremely important parts of the avian diagnostic workup. In seriously ill birds, such testing should be conducted as quickly as possible. In-house microbiology is ideal, for the sooner results are generated the quicker proper therapy can begin. Bacterial culture does, however, have limitations: Some potential pathogens fail to grow on conventional media, such as *Chlamydia,* mycobacteria, megabacteria, and anaerobes, and others are present in low numbers or intermittently shed, such as *Salmonella.*[1]

The normal alimentary tract microbial flora in pet birds is composed of anaerobes and gram-positive bacteria.[1] Normal aerobic bacilli include *Lactobacillus, Corynebacterium,* and *Bacillus.*[1] Normal aerobic cocci include nonhemolytic *Streptococcus, Micrococcus,* and many *Staphylococcus* species, except for *Staphylococcus aureus.*[1] The normal anaerobic flora, in contrast, is poorly characterized.[1]

It should be noted that normal microbial flora varies from species to species. Canaries and finches, for example, often have sparse normal flora. It should also be noted that cultures that lack aerobic growth can occur in normal birds.[1] Gram-negative bacteria are generally considered to be abnormal; however, their presence does not always indicate treatment.[1] Birds can tolerate small numbers and certain strains of *Escherichia coli,* and *Enterobacter,* when present, may be harmless.[1]

Aminoglycosides

Aminoglycosides are bactericidal, are confined to the extracellular space, poorly penetrate the eye and central nervous system,[1] and are excreted through the kidneys. They are not absorbed from the gastrointestinal tract, so they must be administered parenterally.[1] They are relatively toxic in relation to other antibiotics, potentially causing nephrotoxicity, ototoxicity, and other neurologic dysfunction.[1] Thus, they should be used with caution in dehydrated birds or birds with renal disease.

Aminoglycosides have excellent activity against most gram-negative bacteria and *Staphylococcus* but poor activity against most *Streptococcus* and anaerobes.[1] Gentamicin, tobramycin, and amikacin are the aminoglycosides commonly used in avian practice. Amikacin is preferred, as it is the least nephrotoxic.[1] Gentamicin can be used to reduce expense or to treat amikacin-resistant organisms.[1] It is available in several topical ophthalmic preparations that are useful in pet birds. Due to the nephrotoxicity of gentamicin, the condition of a bird under treatment should be carefully monitored. Tobramycin has good activity against *Pseudomonas*.[1]

Aminoglycosides are synergistic with penicillins and cephalosporins, so both groups of drugs are potentiated when they are used in combination.[4] Treatment with aminoglycosides can be administered once or twice a day. As noted above, the drawbacks for their usage are their potential nephrotoxicity and the need to use parenteral administration.[1]

Cephalosporins

Cephalosporins are bactericidal and are widely distributed to the extracellular space but poorly penetrate the central nervous system.[1] They are excreted through the kidneys and are considered less toxic than many other antibiotics.[1] Their low toxicity is advantageous for birds with compromised hepatic or renal function.

Cephalosporins are classified into first-, second-, and third-generation products, with differing spectra of activity.[1] Cephalothin and cephalexin are first-generation antibiotics and are effective against many gram-positive and some gram-negative bacteria.[1] The later generations have increased activity against gram-negative bacteria but reduced activity against gram-positive bacteria.[1] Cefotaxime is effective against *Pseudomonas* and has a further advantage of being able to penetrate the blood-brain barrier, thereby achieving therapeutic levels in the central nervous system.[1] Cefotaxime is synergistic with aminoglycosides, so both drugs are potentiated when used in combination.[4] A disadvantage to cephalosporin use is the frequent dosing required to maintain therapeutic levels.[1]

Enrofloxacin

Enrofloxacin is bactericidal, widely distributed, and excreted primarily through the kidneys.[1] It is well tolerated orally, but intramuscular injections can be irritating.[1] It is one of only a few antibiotics that are effective when administered in the drinking water.[1]

Highly effective against most gram-negative bacteria and some gram-positive bacteria with once or twice daily dosing, enrofloxacin has no activity against anaerobes.[1] Unfortunately, many avian practitioners overuse enrofloxacin, employing it for almost any disease condition. A disadvantage of enrofloxacin is its relative inactivity against many *Streptococcus* spp. and all anaerobes.[1] Another problem is that it is unpalatable, so that birds will refuse oral administration.[1] Disguising the taste with fruit juice or some type of flavoring is sometimes helpful for acceptance.[1]

Penicillins

Penicillins are bactericidal and widely distributed to the extracellular space but poorly penetrate the central nervous system.[1] They are excreted through the kidneys and are considered less toxic than many other antibiotics.[1] As with cephalosporins, their low toxicity is advantageous for birds with compromised hepatic or renal function.

The spectrum of activity and route of administration vary with the particular penicillin drug.[1] Ampicillin and amoxicillin are available in both oral and injectable forms and are effective against many gram-positive but few gram-negative organisms.[1] Later generation penicillins such as ticarcillin and piperacillin have effectiveness against gram-negative bacteria, including *Pseudomonas,* as well as gram-positive bacteria, but are available in injectable form only.[1] Early generation penicillins are not very effective for most avian pathogens, but later generation penicillins with their enhanced effectiveness against gram-negative bacteria are more useful.[1]

When penicillins are used in combination with an aminoglycoside, such as amikacin, potentiation of both drugs occurs.[4] A disadvantage to the use of penicillins is the frequent dosing required to maintain therapeutic levels.[1]

Tetracyclines

Tetracyclines are bacteriostatic with wide tissue distribution.[1] Unlike most other antibiotics, the route of excretion varies from drug to drug.[1] Oral preparations have reduced absorption in the presence of calcium and magnesium.[1] Injectable forms can be irritating and cause necrosis at the injection site.[1] Long-term treatment may lead to immunosuppression and lower the normal gut flora, leading to the development of opportunistic infections, such as candidiasis.[1]

Tetracyclines can be used for a variety of organisms, but their primary use in avian medicine is for the treatment of chlamydiosis, with doxycycline being the drug of choice.[1] Unlike most tetracyclines, doxycycline is minimally affected by calcium, and fungal overgrowth is less likely.[4] Treatment of chlamydiosis has been accomplished through injectables, oral dosing, and addition to food and water with variable success.[1] Tetracyclines can be used in combination with bactericidal drugs to treat bacterial septicemia and chlamydiosis.[4]

Trimethoprim-Sulfonamide Combinations

Trimethoprim-sulfonamide combination drugs are bacteriostatic, have good tissue penetration,[1] and are excreted through the kidneys. Careful monitoring should be conducted, since sulfonamides can cause renal damage in dehydrated birds.[1]

Trimethoprim-sulfonamide combinations have good efficacy against many gram-positive and gram-negative bacteria except for *Pseudomonas*.[1] They are available in oral and injectable forms. The oral form is usually tolerated well; however, some birds may develop gastrointestinal upset or vomiting after administration, particularly macaws.[1] The injectable form can cause irritation at the injection site.[1] Trimethoprim-sulfamethoxazole is the most common combination of drugs in this category used in birds, as it has excellent broad-spectrum activity.[1] The main disadvantages to trimethoprim-sulfonamide combinations are their potential to cause regurgitation and the possibility of renal damage in debilitated birds.[1]

Antifungal Agents

Fungal diseases are among the most frustrating avian infections to diagnose and treat.[5] *Aspergillus* is found throughout the environment, and quite often aspergillosis is the result of poor husbandry practices. Chronic fungal diseases involving *Aspergillus* spp. and *Candida albicans* are often due to immunosuppression.[5] Occasionally, secondary bacterial infections complicate the condition. Due to the nature of the fungal organisms and the pathological changes they produce in the tissues, it is difficult to achieve therapeutic levels of antifungal agents in affected tissues, decreasing treatment success.[5] Thus, treatment of fungal infections requires long-term therapy and is expensive. With the use of newer antifungal drugs, such as itraconazole, better success has been achieved in treatment. Due to the potential side effects

7

of antifungal agents, the general health status of the bird should be carefully monitored.[5]

Antiparasitic Agents

The misuse of antiparasitic and antiprotozoal drugs, especially in poultry, has resulted in many effective drugs being removed from the market.[5] Most dosages for drugs that are available were developed for poultry. Since some of these drugs can be toxic, close supervision of a bird during treatment is important.[5] Droppings should be checked to be certain that the bird is free from parasites. Management of the environment, in addition to drug therapy, is an important part of the treatment plan. Reduction in vermin and vector contact with birds, a clean aviary, quarantine, and post-purchase physical examination of new birds are important to maintain an aviary free of parasites.[5]

Nebulizing Agents

Nebulization therapy is an effective treatment for respiratory disease in pet birds. Air sacculitis is difficult to treat in pet birds: Because of the poor blood supply in birds' air sacs, most drugs administered orally or parenterally fail to reach therapeutic levels. Nebulization can deliver therapeutic agents into the lungs and air sacs, thereby facilitating treatment. Bacterial and fungal infection regimens are often enhanced with the use of nebulization.

Psychotropic Agents

Behavioral problems in avian medicine are frustrating for the practitioner and bird owner alike. Over the past few years, there has been an increasing trend to control such problems as feather picking and other unwanted behaviors with psychotropic agents. The use of these drugs has been based on work with mammals and usage in pet birds by avian practitioners. Psychotropic agents should be used with caution due to their many potential side effects. Medical causes for any behavioral abnormalities should be explored and behavior modification techniques employed before psychotropic agents are administered.

Topical Agents

Topical medications should be used cautiously and applied sparingly. Any preparation, especially creams and ointments, that is applied too heavily or carelessly can be rapidly distributed throughout the feathers as the bird preens, resulting in oily, greasy, or matted feathers.[4] This decreases the insulative property of the feathers and may result in feather loss. Ointments and creams should not be applied directly on the feathers. Instead, they should be applied conservatively to unfeathered parts of the body.[4] If a lesion must be treated in a feathered area, the medication should be applied carefully and treatment should be stopped if the feathers become oily or greasy.[4] Application of mild detergents can remove these medications from the feathers.[4] Ophthalmic ointments should be used sparingly to avoid feather loss around the eyes. Any excess medication around the margins of the eyes should be blotted up.

Avian Drug Dosages

ANTIMICROBIAL AGENTS

DRUG DOSAGE AND ROUTE   COMMENTS

Acyclovir

80 mg/kg q 8h PO[4,6,7] or
20–40 mg/kg q 12h IM[4]

Antiviral agent commonly used to treat
Pacheco's disease. Can be mixed with food
(up to 240 mg/kg of food) or drinking water
(1 mg/ml drinking water). With all routes of
administration, most effective if initiated before
onset of clinical signs. IM injection causes
severe muscle necrosis.

Amikacin

10–15 mg/kg q 12h IM, IV[3,4,8]

Good-spectrum antibiotic. Less toxic than
gentamicin. Nephrotoxicity increased in
dehydrated patients. Synergistic effect with
third-generation penicillins.

Amoxicillin

150–175 mg/kg q 6h PO or
150 mg/kg q 6h IM[3]

Not effective against most common avian
pathogens. Injectable form effective for
treatment of cat bites.

Amoxicillin–clavulanic acid

150 mg/kg q 8h PO[9]

Broader range of activity than amoxicillin.
Effective against penicillinase-producing
organisms. Used for treatment of sinus and
skin infections.

IC = intracardially
IM = intramuscularly
IO = intraosseously
IT = intratracheally
IV = intravenously
PO = per os; orally
SC = subcutaneously

Ampicillin
100 mg/kg q 4h IM[3,10] or   Not effective against most avian pathogens.
100–200 mg/kg q 6–8h PO[3]   Injectable form effective for treatment of cat
                                       bites.

Azithromycin
40 mg/kg q 24h PO[11]   Proposed treatment for chlamydiosis. Five-day-
                                       on, five-day-off regimen for 45 days.

Carbenicillin
100 mg/kg q 8h IM[12] or
100 mg/kg q 12h PO[13]

Cefadroxil
100 mg/kg q 12h PO[2]   Palatable, broad-spectrum cephalosporin.

Cefazolin
50–75 mg/kg q 12h IM[2]   Broad-spectrum antimicrobial.

Cefotaxime
75–100 mg/kg q 6–8h IM,   Good broad-spectrum antimicrobial with activity
IV[3,12]   against many gram-negative and gram-positive
                                       organisms. Penetrates the blood-brain barrier.

Ceftazidime
75–100 mg/kg q 6–8h IM, IV[13] Broad-spectrum antimicrobial; able to penetrate
                                       blood-brain barrier.

Ceftiofur
50–100 mg/kg q 6h IM[5]   Broad-spectrum third-generation cephalosporin.

Ceftriaxone
75–100 mg/kg q 6–8h IM, IV[3]

Cephalexin
50–100 mg/kg q 6–8h PO[13]   Effective against many gram-positive and some
                                       gram-negative organisms. Good for treating
                                       staph dermatitis. Palatable.

continued

11

Cephalothin

100 mg/kg q 6h IM, IV[10,13]

Painful injection. Not absorbed from gastrointestinal tract.

Chloramphenicol

50–70 mg/kg chloramphenicol palmitate q 6–8h PO[12] or 50 mg/kg chloramphenicol succinate q 8h IM[3]

Good tissue penetration, but bacteriostatic nature limits effectiveness. Activity against some gram-positive and gram-negative organisms. Human health concern; avoid skin contact. Chloramphenicol palmitate can be compounded commercially.

Chlorhexidine

10–30 ml/gal. drinking water[3]
Topical: 0.5% solution[3]

Some effectiveness against gram-negative bacteria and yeast. Not recommended for use with finches. Never studied for use internally. Topical use as wound lavage.

Chlortetracycline

In feed: 1% in pelleted food or 0.5% in millet for 45 days[3,4]
PO: 1,000–1,500 mg/L drinking water or 1,500 mg/kg soft food for 45 days[3,4]

Used for treatment of chlamydiosis. Doxycycline is more effective. *Candida* overgrowth possible.

Ciprofloxacin

15–20 mg/kg q 12h PO, IM,[12] or 250 mg/L drinking water for 5–10 days[14]

Broad-spectrum antibiotic. An oral 50 mg/ml suspension can be made by crushing a 500-mg tablet in 10 ml water.

Clindamycin

100 mg/kg q 24h PO[3]
For treatment of osteomyelitis: 150 mg/kg q 24h PO[2]

Effective against gram-positive and anaerobic organisms.

Doxycycline (Vibramycin)

Cockatiels and amazons: 40–50 mg/kg q 12–24h PO[3,15]

African greys, cockatoos, and macaws: 25 mg/kg q 12–24h PO[3,15]

Drug of choice for treatment of chlamydiosis. Less risk of *Candida* overgrowth than with other tetracyclines. 45-day treatment period. Also activity against *Mycoplasma* and many gram-positive organisms. Macaws are sensitive to this drug and may regurgitate following oral administration.

Doxycycline (Vibravenos)

Macaws: 75–100 mg/kg IM once, then weekly for 6–7 injections[3,15]

Other psittacines: 25–50 mg/kg IM once, then weekly for 6–7 injections[3,15]

Long-acting injectable for treatment of chlamydiosis. Not available in U.S. Large volume of injection requires multiple injection sites.

Doxycycline hyclate

Cockatiels: 500 mg/kg hulled seed or 200 mg/L drinking water[16]

Other psittacines: 1,000 mg/kg soft food[16]

Suggested treatment for chlamydiosis. Cockatiels require lower dose in food or water as toxicosis can result.

Enrofloxacin

7.5–15 mg/kg q 12–24h PO, IM[3,12]

Injectable can also be used orally, but not palatable. Tablets can be crushed in syrup to disguise taste. Broad spectrum of activity against most gram-negative and some gram-positive bacteria and against *Mycoplasma*. Little evidence of development of joint problems in young birds due to use.

continued

13

Erythromycin
PO: 10–20 mg/kg q 12h[3]
Soluble powder: 500 mg/gal.
  drinking water[3]
IM: 60 mg/kg q 12h[12]

May be effective against *Mycoplasma* and chronic respiratory tract infections.

Gentamicin
2.5 mg/kg q 12h IM[12]

Not used often in birds due to its nephrotoxicity and the effectiveness of amikacin. Still used in nebulization therapy.

Kanamycin
10–20 mg/kg q 12h IM[17]

Used for treatment of enteric infections. Not used frequently due to nephrotoxicity.

Lincocin-spectinomycin
Water-soluble powder:
  1/8–1/4 tsp./16 oz. drinking
  water for 10–14 days[10]

Combination of two antibiotics in water-soluble powder.

Lincomycin
75 mg/kg q 12h PO[10] or
  1/8–1/4 tsp./16 oz. drinking
  water[10]

For treatment of chronic upper respiratory tract infections, *Mycoplasma,* and chronic dermatitis.

Metronidazole
10–30 mg/kg q 12h for
  10 days PO[3,18]
100 mg/L drinking water or
  100 mg/kg soft food[19]
10 mg/kg q 24h for 2 days
  IM[3,20]

Some effectiveness against anaerobic bacterial infections. Used for protozoal infections caused by *Giardia, Trichomonas,* and *Hexamita.* Not recommended for use in finches.

Nitrofurazone (9.2% powder)
1 tsp./gal. drinking water[3,13]

May be hepatotoxic. Not recommended for use in finches or pigeons. Mynahs and lories should receive half dosage (1/2 tsp./gal.).

Oxytetracycline
58 mg/kg q 24h IM[3,7,12]
Cockatoos: 50–100 mg/kg q
2–3 days SC, IM[3,12]

Some activity against *Chlamydia*. Injections can
cause severe muscle necrosis.

Piperacillin
100–200 mg/kg q 6–8h IM,
IV[3,4,12]

Great broad-spectrum antibiotic. Synergistic
with aminoglycosides. Effective against many
gram-negative, gram-positive, anaerobic, and
resistant *Pseudomonas* spp.

Rifampin
10–20 mg/kg q 12h PO[3,4]

Treatment for avian tuberculosis. Possible toxic
side effects. Treatment is long term, often
extending over several months.

Sulfachlorpyridazine
1/4–1 tsp./L drinking water[3,5]

Effective against enteric infections and *E. coli*.
Bitter taste causes poor acceptance. Can
disguise taste with fruit juice or sugar.

Tetracycline
Soluble powder (10 g/6.4 oz.):
200 mg/gal. drinking water
for 5–10 days[10]
Suspension/solution
(100 mg/ml): 200–250
mg/kg q 12h PO[3,17]

Limited effectiveness. Can develop secondary
Candida overgrowth.

Ticarcillin
150–200 mg/kg q 6–8h IM,
IV[3,21]

Broad-spectrum antibiotic. Synergistic with
aminoglycosides. Activity against gram-
negative, gram-positive, anaerobic, and
Pseudomonas organisms.

continued

15

Tobramycin

2.5–5 mg/kg q 12h IM[3,4,10]   Used for highly resistant strains of
Pseudomonas. Use with caution due to
nephrotoxicity.

**Trimethoprim-
sulfamethoxazole**

96 mg/kg q 12h (2 ml/kg) PO,[4]   Broad-spectrum antibiotic. May be regurgitated
16–24 mg/kg q 12h PO,[3] or   by some birds. Good for treating respiratory
48 mg/120 ml drinking water[2]   and enteric infections.

**Tylosin (250 g/8.8 oz.
solution)**

1/2 tsp./gal. drinking water[2]   Effective against some respiratory tract
infections and *Mycoplasma*. Bitter taste.

ANTIFUNGAL AGENTS

DRUG DOSAGE AND ROUTE   COMMENTS

Amphotericin B

1.5 mg/kg q 8–12h IV for   For treatment of aspergillosis. Possibly
3 days[3,4,21] or 1 mg/kg q nephrotoxic.
8–12h IT[3,4,22,23]

**Chlorhexidine
(20 mg/ml solution)**

10–25 ml/gal. drinking   Preventative or treatment for gastrointestinal
water[4,13]   *Candida*. Can be toxic to finches.

Clotrimazole

0.2 ml/kg q 24h for 5 days IT[2]   Adjunct for *Aspergillus* therapy. Topical used at
or 10 mg/ml topical flush[23]   sites that can be flushed in early infections.

Fluconazole

2–5 mg/kg q 24h for 7–10 days PO[3,4,24] or 5–15 mg/kg q 12h for 14–60 days PO[2]

Used for treatment of systemic candidiasis. May be regurgitated by some birds. Has safest therapeutic index of azole antifungals. Less effective than itraconazole in treating aspergillosis but has been used for that purpose. Due to penetration ability, recommended for treating central nervous system infections.

Flucytosine

20–50 mg/kg q 12h for 21 days PO[3]

Has been used to treat aspergillosis in conjunction with amphotericin B. Can be useful in treatment of systemic candidiasis.

Itraconazole

5–10 mg/kg q 12h for 4–5 weeks PO[3,25]

African greys: 5 mg/kg q 24h PO[3,25]

Drug of choice for treating aspergillosis. Very effective and less toxic than other antifungals, but expensive. Available in suspension and capsules. If capsules are used, dissolve 1 capsule in 2 ml of 0.1N HCl (stable for 7 days), then dilute in 18 ml orange juice and dose accordingly. African greys are sensitive to this drug. Do not use with central nervous system infections.

Ketoconazole

20–30 mg/kg q 12h for 21 days PO[3,4,23]

For treatment of systemic candidiasis. Tablets can be crushed and added to orange or pineapple juice, lactulose, or 1M HCl and water.

Miconazole (1 or 2%)

Use topically, as needed[4]

Can be used to treat topical fungal infections.

continued

17

Nystatin (100,000 units/ml)

1 ml/300 g q 8–12h PO or
1 ml/L drinking water[3,4,17]

Very safe, as not absorbed systemically. Effective against gastrointestinal candidiasis only, since it must come in contact with lesions. Large doses are best given by gavage.

STA solution

Use topically, as needed[3]

Used as a topical treatment for fungal dermatitis.

ANTHELMINTIC/ANTIPARASITIC AGENTS

DRUG DOSAGE AND ROUTE   COMMENTS

Amprolium (9.6% solution)

2–4 ml/gal. drinking water for 5–7 days[3,26]

For control of coccidiosis. Environment should be cleaned to prevent reinfection.

Carbaryl 5% powder

Topical: Lightly dust feathers[3,21,26]

Safe treatment for some ectoparasites.

Nest box: 1–2 tsp., depending on size of box[3,21,26]

Use as needed to control parasites in environment. Remove after 24 hours.

Carnidazole

Adults: 200 mg/kg PO, once[3,27]

Young: 100 mg/kg PO, once[3,27]

Antiprotozoal for treatment of *Trichomonas, Hexamita,* and *Histomonas* in pigeons. Can be used for *Giardia* in cockatiels. May need to repeat treatment in 10–14 days. Wide margin of safety.

Chlorsulon

20 mg/kg PO, three times, 2 weeks apart[3]

For treatment of flukes and tapeworms.

Clazuril

5–10 mg/kg q 24h for 3 days PO, then 2 days off, then treat for another 3 days[3,26]

High efficacy as coccidiostat for poultry and pigeons.

Crotamiton

Topical[21]

Apply to affected areas to treat topical mite infestations, such as *Knemidokoptes*. Use in combination with ivermectin therapy.

Dimetridazole

1 tsp./gal. drinking water[3,13,26]
Lories: 1/2 tsp./gal. drinking water[3]

Antiprotozoal for treatment of *Giardia, Hexamita, Trichomonas,* and *Histomonas.* Low therapeutic index. Not available in the U.S. Not recommended in finches.

Fenbendazole

For treatment of ascarids: 20–50 mg/kg PO, repeat in 10 days[3]
For treatment of flukes and microfilaria: 20–50 mg/kg *q* 24h for 3 days PO[3]
For treatment of *Capillaria:* 20–50 mg/kg *q* 24h for 5 days PO[3]

Has been used to treat ascarids, flukes, microfilaria, and *Capillaria.* There is a low margin of safety. Cockatiels are especially sensitive. Toxicity has also been reported in canaries, pigeons, and quail.

Ipronidazole

500 mg/gal. drinking water for 7–30 days[3,4]

Used for treatment of protozoa, *Giardia, Hexamita, Trichomonas,* and *Histomonas.* Not available in the U.S.

Ivermectin

200 μg/kg PO, SC, IM, repeat in 10–14 days, or use topically[3,4,28]

Used for treatment of nematodes, lice, and mites. Treatment of choice for *Knemidokoptes*. May be toxic to finches and waxbills. Can dilute with saline for immediate use or with propylene glycol for extended use.

continued

19

Levamisole (13.65%)

5 mg/kg IM; repeat in 14 days[3]
Flock treatment: 5–15 ml/gal.
drinking water for 1 to 3
days[3,4]

Treatment for nematodes. Also has immunomodulating effects. Low therapeutic index. IM injection may cause reaction.

Mebendazole

25 mg/kg q 24h for 5 days
PO[4,21]

Treatment for nematodes, some tapeworms, and flukes. *Capillaria* are sensitive to this drug. Do not use during breeding season.

Metronidazole

10–30 mg/kg q 12h for
10 days PO[3,18]
100–400 mg/L drinking water
or 100 mg/kg soft food[19]
10 mg/kg q 24h for 2 days
IM[3,20]

Some effectiveness against anaerobic bacterial infections. Used to treat protozoal infections caused by *Giardia, Trichomonas,* and *Hexamita.* Use with caution in finches.

Niclosamide

50 mg/kg via gavage; repeat
in 10–14 days[4,26]

Tapeworm treatment. Rarely used due to better efficacy and ease of use of praziquantel.

Oxfendazole

10–40 mg/kg PO; single
dose[26]

Treatment for nematodes. Do not use during breeding season.

Praziquantel

PO: 10–20 mg/kg; repeat in
10–14 days[3,13]
IM: Flukes—9 mg/kg q 24h for
3 days, then oral
administration for 11 days.[3]
Tapeworms—9 mg/kg once;
repeat in 10–14 days[3]

Treatment for tapeworms and flukes. Injectable may be toxic to finches.

Pyrantel pamoate

4.5 mg/kg PO; repeat in 10–14 days[3,4,21]

Treatment for gastrointestinal nematodes.

Pyrethrin products (0.150%)

Topical: Lightly mist feathers[3]

Treatment for ectoparasites that are resistant to carbaryl (mainly lice).

Pyrimethamine

0.5 mg/kg q 12h PO (Mix tablet with 21 ml water and 4 ml KY jelly for 1 mg/ml suspension)[3,29]

Treatment for *Plasmodium, Sarcocystis,* and *Toxoplasma.* Use in combination with trimethoprim-sulfamethoxazole for *Sarcocystis.*

Quinacrine

5–10 mg/kg q 24h for 7 days PO[3]

A treatment for *Plasmodium* in psittacines.

Pigeons: 100–300 mg/gal. drinking water for 10–21 days[30]

Ronidazole

6–10 mg/kg q 24h for 6–10 days PO[31] or 400 mg/gal. drinking water for 3–5 days[26]

Effective against *Giardia, Trichomonas, Histomonas,* and other protozoa. Wide margin of safety. Limited U.S. availability. Drug of choice for *Trichomonas* in pigeons.

Sulfadimethoxine (12.5% solution)

25 mg/kg q 12h for 5 days PO[2]

Treatment for coccidiosis.

continued

Thiabendazole
For treatment of ascarids:
250–500 mg/kg PO; repeat
in 10–14 days[3,21]
For treatment of *Syngamus:*
100 mg/kg PO *q* 24h for
7–10 days[3,21]

NEBULIZING AGENTS

DRUG DOSAGE AND ROUTE	COMMENTS
Acetylcysteine (20% solution) 200 mg/9 ml sterile water,[2] 200 mg/8 ml sterile water + 1 ml amikacin or gentocin,[2] or 2–5 drops in nebulizing solution[21]	Mucolytic. Used in treatment for rhinitis, pneumonia, and air sacculitis. Can cause tracheal irritation. Mix with dexamethasone, aminoglycosides, and aminophylline. Neonates may be sensitive.
Amikacin 50 mg/9 ml sterile water[2]	Used in treatment of rhinitis, pneumonia, and air sacculitis.
Aminophylline 25 mg/9 ml sterile water or saline for 15 minutes[2]	Bronchodilator. Can mix with dexamethasone, aminoglycosides, and acetylcysteine.
Amphotericin B 1 mg/ml sterile water for 15 minutes *q* 12h[2,10]	Antifungal agent.
Carbenicillin 200 mg/9 ml saline[2]	Used for *Pseudomonas* respiratory tract infections in combination with systemic treatment.
Chloramphenicol 100 mg/9 ml saline or sterile water for 15 minutes[2]	

Clotrimazole

1% solution for 30–60 minutes[2]

Antifungal used in combination with systemic antifungal.

Erythromycin

1 ml injectable solution/10 ml saline q 8h[3]

Gentamicin

50 mg/9 ml sterile water for 15 minutes or 50 mg/8 ml sterile water + 1 ml 20% acetylcysteine[2]

Used in treatment of rhinitis, pneumonia, and air sacculitis.

Tylosin

1 g powder/50 ml distilled water for 60 minutes[2]

For treatment of respiratory tract infections in pigeons and quails.

PSYCHOTROPIC AGENTS

DRUG DOSAGE AND ROUTE   COMMENTS

Amitriptyline

1–2 mg/kg q 12–24h PO[3,4]

Antidepressant that causes mood elevation. Many side effects. Used for behavioral feather picking, but not usually effective.

Carbamazepine

3–10 mg/kg PO[2]

Anticonvulsant. Also used in obsessive-compulsive disorder. For the latter, use in combination with chlorpromazine or haloperidol for initial 2 weeks. Can cause hepatomegaly and bone marrow suppression.

Clomipramine hydrochloride

0.5–1.0 mg/kg q 12–24h PO[4,32,33]

Antidepressant with many side effects. Treatment for feather picking and self-mutilation in psittacines. Start with low dose and gradually increase over 4 to 5 days.

continued

23

Doxepin
0.5–1.0 mg/kg q 12h PO[4,33]

Antidepressant. Useful in some cases of feather picking. May cause severe depression or lethargy.

Fluoxetine
1–2 mg/kg q 12h PO[33]

Antidepressant used as adjunct treatment for depression-induced feather picking.

Haloperidol
Initial dose: 0.2 mg/kg q 12–24h PO if < 1 kg; 0.15 mg/kg q 12–24h PO if > 1 kg[3,4]

Treatment for feather picking and self-mutilation. Following initial dose, increase by 0.01 ml every 2 days. Discontinue treatment if ataxia, anorexia, or vomiting develops.

Naltrexone
1.5 mg q 12h PO[33,34]

Narcotic antagonist used to treat endorphin addiction. Also used to treat feather picking and self-mutilation.

Nortriptyline
2 mg/120 ml drinking water[3,4,35]

Antidepressant that causes mood elevation. May be effective in treating some cases of feather picking or self-mutilation. Dose should be decreased or discontinued if hyperactivity develops.

TOPICAL AGENTS FOR OPHTHALMIC AND DERMATOLOGIC CONDITIONS
DRUG DOSAGE AND ROUTE   COMMENTS

Acemannan
Topical[36]

Hydrogel. Stimulates healing of open wounds.

Aloe vera
Topical[3]

To use as spray, mix 0.5 oz./pint of water or mix 0.5 oz. with 1 pint water, 1 tsp. Penetran, and 2 drops of Woolite. Soothes irritated skin. Aids in feather-picking treatment.

Ammonium solution
Topical[3]   Analgesic, antipruritic ointment.

Bacitracin/Neomycin/
Polymixin
Intraocular/intranasal/topical;   Combination antibiotic ointment.
  use q 8–12h[4]

Chloramphenicol
Intraocular/intranasal/topical;   Effective ocular ointment.
  use q 8–12h

Chloramphenicol–
prednisolone acetate
Intraocular/intranasal/topical;   Effective antibiotic/steroid combination
  use q 8–12h[4]   ointment. Possible cortisone absorption.

Ferric subsulfate
Topical[3]   Apply as needed to control hemorrhaging.

Gentamicin sulfate
Intraocular/intranasal/topical;   Various forms, including ointment and drops.
  use q 8–12h[4]

Gentamicin sulfate–
betamethasone
Intraocular/intranasal/topical;   Antibiotic/steroid combination drops. Possible
  use q 8–12h[4]   cortisone absorption.

Neomycin
Intraocular/intranasal/topical;   Antibiotic ointment.
  use q 8–12h[3]

continued

25

**Neomycin sulfate–
isoflupredone
acetate–tetracaine
hydrochloride**
Intraocular/intranasal/topical;   Topical antibiotic, steroid, and topical anesthetic
use *q* 12–24h[4]   combination. Possible cortisone absorption.

**Oxytetracycline hydro-
chloride with polymixin B**
Intraocular/intranasal/topical;   More specific topical agent for chlamydiosis and
use *q* 8–12h   *Mycoplasma.* Use with systemic drugs.

Yeast cell derivatives
Topical; use as needed[5]   Stimulates epithelial healing, including
                                  abrasions and lacerations. Aids in treatment
                                  of nonhealing wounds.

MISCELLANEOUS AGENTS

DRUG DOSAGE AND ROUTE   COMMENTS

**Acetaminophen (325 mg
elixir concentration)**
0.15 ml elixir/L drinking water[5]   Analgesic.

**Acetylsalicylic acid
(aspirin; 325 mg tablet)**
1 tablet/250 ml drinking   For control of pain and inflammation;
water[3,21,37]   anticoagulant.

ACTH gel
1–2 IU/kg IM[4]   For ACTH stimulation test.

Allopurinol
Stock solution: Crush 100 mg   For articular gout. Maintain good hydration.
in 10 ml water. Mix 1 ml per
ounce of drinking water or
give 10 mg/kg orally *q*
4–12h[13,38]

Aminopentamide

0.05 mg/kg q 12h IM, SC; 5 doses maximum[3]
Antiemetic, antidiarrheal, slows gastrointestinal motility.

Aminophylline

4 mg/kg q 6–12h PO[2]
10 mg/kg q 3h IV[2]
Bronchodilator with diuretic and vasodilation effects. Give orally after initial response.

Atropine

0.5 mg/kg IM, IV, IO, IT[2]
Cardiopulmonary resuscitation.

0.01–0.02 mg/kg SC, IM[3,39]
Preanesthetic. Rarely used; secretions may thicken and occlude airway.

0.2 mg/kg q 3–4h IM, IV[40]
For treatment of organophosphate toxicity.

Bismuth sulfate

1ml/kg q 8–12h PO[4,41]
Weak adsorbent, demulcent.

Butorphanol tartrate

3–4 mg/kg as needed PO, IM, IV[3,42]
Analgesic, antitussive.

Calcium disodium versenate (Calcium EDTA)

35 mg/kg q 12h IM[13,40,41] or 20–40 mg/kg q 8–12h IM[3]
Chelating agent for heavy metal (lead, zinc) toxicosis. Can cause renal tubular necrosis. Discontinue if polyuria develops.

Charcoal (activated), kaolin

2–8 mg/kg as needed, PO[3,4,41]
Adsorbs toxins. Use 1 g/5–10 ml water

Cimetidine

5–10 mg/kg q 8–12h PO[4] or 300 mg/5 ml drinking water[3]
For treatment of gastric ulceration.

Cisapride

1 mg/kg q 12h PO[5]
Gastrointestinal stimulant for motility problems. Very effective for gut stasis in neonates.

continued

27

Colchicine (with probenecid)

0.04 mg/kg q 24h PO; can gradually increase to q 12h[4,43]

For treatment of gout and hepatic fibrosis. Discontinue if vomiting or diarrhea occurs.

Deferoxamine

100 mg/kg q 24h SC[44]

Iron chelator, for treatment of hemachromatosis.

Dexamethasone

2–4 mg/kg q 8–24h IM, IV[13,45]

Anti-inflammatory agent. Use higher dose (4 mg/kg) for shock and head trauma.

Dexamethasone sodium phosphate

2–4 mg/kg q 12h IM, IV[2]

Used in head trauma and shock cases.

Dextrose (5–50% solution)

50–100 mg/kg SC, IM, IV, slowly to effect[4]

For treatment of hypoglycemia. Give IV solution slowly. Use 5% solution SC or IM.

Diazepam

0.5–1 mg/kg q 8–12h IM, IV, as needed[3,21] or 2.5–4 mg/kg PO as needed[3]

For sedation, seizure control, tranquilizing, or appetite stimulation. Used to treat feather picking and for calming effect.

Digoxin

0.01–0.02 mg/kg q 12–24h PO[4]

For treatment of congestive heart failure and cardiomyopathy. Monitor ECG.

Dimercaprol

25–35 mg/kg q 12h PO, 5 days a week for 2–5 weeks[4]

Chelating agent. Less toxic than calcium EDTA.

Dimercaptosuccinic acid (DMSA)

30 mg/kg q 12h PO[46,47]

Oral chelator for zinc and lead toxicity.

Dinoprost tromethamine
0.02–0.1 mg/kg once; IM,
intracloacally[3,4]

Prostaglandin F2 alpha. May facilitate egg passage when the egg is in oviduct. Can cause oviduct rupture.

Diphenhydramine hydrochloride
1–4 mg/kg q 8h PO[3,21] or
1–2 ml/120 ml drinking water[4]

Used in feather pickers and highly stressed birds. Also used as treatment for allergic sinusitis.

Dipyrone (50% solution)
25 mg/kg q 8–12h IM, IV[4]

Reduces fever in toxemia cases.

Docusate sodium (50 mg/ml syrup)
1 ml/oz. drinking water[48]

Laxative. Aids in expelling lead from ventriculus.

Doxapram
5–10 mg/kg once; SC, IM, IV[3]

Respiratory stimulant.

Echinacea
2.5 drops/kg PO or 5 drops/cup drinking water[3]

Immunostimulant. May speed recovery in debilitated birds.

Epinephrine (1:1,000)
0.1 mg/kg IV, IT, IC, IO[3]

For cardiopulmonary resuscitation (CPR).

Ferric subsulfate
Topical, as needed[3]

For hemostasis of nails or beak.

Fludrocortisone
1/2 tablet/4 oz. drinking water[4]

Used in adrenal replacement therapy.

Flunixin meglumine
1–10 mg/kg IM, IV[3,4,21]

Anti-inflammatory, analgesic. May cause vomiting and diarrhea.

continued

Furosemide

0.15–2 mg/kg q 12–24h IM, PO[2,3]

Diuretic. Lories and some other avian species very sensitive. Low margin of safety.

Hemicellulose

Small amount on food daily,[4] 0.5 tsp./60 ml hand-feeding formula or gruel,[40,41] or 1–3% of gavage feeding[40,41]

For bulk in diet. Facilitates defecation in bowel deficit disorders and other conditions.

Human chorionic gonadotropin

250–500 IU/kg IM on days 1, 3, and 7 or once every 4–6 weeks[2,49]

Used to prevent egg laying and in treatment for feather picking. Resistance may develop. Fewer side effects than medroxyprogesterone acetate.

Hydroxyzine

2.0–2.2 mg/kg q 8h PO or 4 mg/100–120 ml drinking water[35]

Used for treatment of respiratory allergies, allergic sinusitis, self-mutilation, and feather picking.

Insulin, NPH

0.5–3 units/kg IM[21]

Treatment for diabetes mellitus. Birds should be closely monitored during treatment. Suggested initial dose for budgerigars is 0.002 U; for larger psittacines, 0.01–0.1 U.

Kaolin-pectin

2 ml/kg q 12h PO[21,45]

Gut protectant.

Lactobacillus

1 pinch/day/bird PO or 1 tsp./qt. hand-feeding formula[3]

Powder used to replace gut flora. Can be used in young and debilitated birds.

Lactulose

0.3 ml/kg *q* 24h PO or divided
q 12h PO[3,4]

Retards absorption of toxins from the gastrointestinal tract. Commonly used with liver failure. Reduces blood ammonia levels. Decrease dose if diarrhea develops. "Liver-sparing" drug.

Levothyroxine

0.02 mg/kg *q* 12–24h PO[13]
0.1 mg tablet/4–12 oz. drinking water[50]

Treatment for hypothyroidism. Monitor long-term therapy. Aids in treating obesity and lipomas. Watch for signs of overdosage.

Mannitol

0.5 mg/kg *q* 24h IV[3,4,46]

Osmotic diuretic used to treat brain edema, especially after head trauma. Administer IV slowly.

Medroxyprogesterone acetate (150 mg/ml)

5–25 mg/kg IM, SC, repeat in 4–6 weeks if needed,[3] or 0.03 ml/100 g (up to 150 g); 0.027 ml/100 g (150–300 g); 0.025 ml/100 g (300–700 g); 0.022 ml/100 g (700+ g)[4]

Suppresses ovulation and calms sexual aggression, but side effects limit usefulness. Reported side effects include weight gain, polyuria/polydipsia, diabetes mellitus, lethargy, thromboemboli, and liver impairment. Controversial drug; use with caution. Administer no more than 2–4 times a year.

Methylprednisolone acetate

0.5–1 mg/kg PO, IM[3]

For allergy problems, immune disorders.

Metoclopramide

0.5 mg/kg *q* 8–12h PO, IM, IV[3,4]

Used for gastrointestinal motility problems (delayed crop emptying, regurgitation, vomiting). Do not use with gastrointestinal foreign body or blockage.

continued

Mibolerone

10 μg/kg q 24h PO or 3–6 drops/oz. drinking water daily[4]

Aids in preventing oviposition.

Mineral oil

0.3 ml/35 g or 3.5 ml/500 g q 12–24h PO[41]

5–10 ml/kg q 12–24h PO[4]

Cathartic. Aids in foreign body removal.

Oxytocin

5 IU/kg IM; may repeat in 30 minutes[51]

Used with calcium gluconate to assist in passage of egg. Contraindicated if uterine rupture, egg is adhered to the oviduct, or passage of egg is mechanically impeded.

Pancreatic enzyme

1/8 tsp./kg food[4,17]

1/8 tsp./1–4 oz. hand-feeding formula for neonates[52]

Treatment for pancreatic insufficiency. May aid in digestion of food.

D-penicillamine

52 mg/kg q 12h for 1–2 weeks PO[3]

Treatment for heavy metal (lead, zinc) toxicosis.

Phenobarbitol

1–5 mg/kg q 8–12h PO[3] or 4–8 mg/120 ml drinking water[4]

Anticonvulsant and sedative. May aid in some feather-picking conditions.

Pralidaxime

10–100 mg/kg q 24–48h IM[40,41,47]

Treatment for organophosphate toxicosis. Use lower dose in combination with atropine.

Prednisolone

0.5–1.0 mg/kg IM, IV[3,21]

Anti-inflammatory agent.

Prednisolone sodium succinate

As anti-inflammatory agent:
0.5–1 mg/kg IM, IV[4]
For CPR or head trauma:
10–20 mg/kg IM, IV[21]
For immunosuppression:
2–4 mg/kg IM, IV[21]

Anti-inflammatory agent. Shock treatment at higher dosages. Immunosuppressive.

Propanolol

0.2 mg/kg IM or 0.04 mg/kg IV[3,4]

Treatment for cardiac dysrhythmias. Administer IV slowly.

Sodium bicarbonate

1 meq/kg IV, IO, q 15–30 minutes to maximum of 4 meq/kg[3]

Treatment for shock and metabolic acidosis.

5 meq/kg IV, IO, once[2]

For CPR.

Sodium sulfate

0.5–1.0 g/kg PO[41] or 2 g/kg slurry for 2 days[3]

Used for treatment of lead toxicosis; cathartic adjunct to chelation. Do not use in cases of impaired gastrointestinal function or dehydration.

Stanozolol
(IM form: 50 mg/ml)

25–50 mg/kg 1–2 times weekly IM[3] or 2 mg/4 oz. drinking water[13]

Used to increase weight in anorectic cases. Exercise caution with hepatic or renal disorders.

Sucralfate

25 mg/kg q 8h PO[3]

Treatment for upper gastrointestinal tract bleeding; protective coating formed in proventriculus. Give 1 hour before food or other drugs.

continued

Testosterone

IM: 8 mg/kg weekly, as needed[13,21]

Drinking water administration: Mix 100 mg in 30 ml of water to make stock solution. Then use 5–10 drops stock solution/30 ml drinking water, mixed fresh daily, for 5–10 days.[2,4]

Used in cases of chronic egg laying. Contraindicated in birds with liver or kidney disease. Used in canaries for decreased libido or to stimulate singing.

Vitamin K$_1$

0.2–2.5 mg/kg q 24h IM, as needed[3]

For warfarin toxicity: 0.2–2.5 mg/kg q 12h IM for 7 days[3]

Treatment for coagulation problems and anticoagulant rodenticide toxicosis.

NUTRITIONAL SUPPORT

DRUG DOSAGE AND ROUTE	COMMENTS

Calcium glubionate (Neo-calglucon)

150 mg/kg q 12h PO or 1 ml/30 ml drinking water[53]

Calcium supplementation.

Calcium gluconate

5–10 mg/kg q 12h SC, IM, as needed[3]

50–100 mg/kg IV, slowly to effect[3]

Used for calcium supplementation. Maintain adequate hydration during usage.

Calcium lactate– glycerophosphate

5–10 mg/kg for 7 days IM, as needed[53]

Calcium supplementation.

Dextrose (5–50% solution)

50–100 mg/kg SC, IM, IV, slowly to effect[4]

Treatment for hypoglycemia. Give IV solution slowly. Use 5% solution for SC or IM administration.

Iodine

Mix 2 ml in 30 ml of water to make stock solution. Then use 1 drop stock solution/30 ml drinking water. Adjust dose to maintenance level as improvement noted. Gradually decrease from daily to weekly.[48]

Treatment for goiter. Mix dilute solution daily.

Iron dextran

10 mg/kg IM; repeat in 7–10 days[3,4]

Treatment for anemia and hemorrhage or iron deficiency. Use cautiously in toucans, mynahs, starlings, and other birds prone to iron storage disease.

Lactobacillus

1 pinch/day/bird PO or 1 tsp./qt. hand-feeding formula[3]

For replacement of normal gut flora.

Osteoform powder

1/8 tsp./kg food[48]

Calcium, phosphorus, and vitamin D_3 supplement.

Sodium iodide (20% solution)

0.3 mg/kg IM[53]

Initial treatment for severe thyroid dysplasia. Continue with oral therapy when improvement noted.

continued

Vitamin A

0.05–0.1 ml/100 g IM

Treatment for hypovitaminosis A and ophthalmic problems; supplement for sinusitis. Administer weekly.

Vitamin A, D$_3$, and E

0.1–0.2 ml/300 g IM[3]

Same uses as for vitamin A. Too frequent usage could lead to renal mineralization due to vitamin D$_3$. Use with caution in macaws.

Vitamin B complex

1–3 mg/kg IM; dosage depends upon thiamine content[3]

Treatment for muscular weakness, debilitation, and anemia. Appetite stimulant. Use as adjunct to therapy in neurological, liver, kidney, and gastrointestinal disease.

Vitamin B$_{12}$ (Cyanocobalamin)

250–500 μg/kg IM[21]

Administer weekly.

Vitamin C (Ascorbic acid)

20–40 mg/kg IM[21]

Support for debilitating metabolic or infectious diseases. Administer weekly.

Vitamin E–selenium

0.06 mg Se/kg every 3–14 days IM, as needed,[53] or 0.05–0.1 mg/kg every 14 days IM[3]

For prevention and treatment of muscular weakness. Also used as treatment for paralysis in cockatiels.

References

1. Flammer, K. Common bacterial infections and antibiotic use in companion birds. Antimicrobial Therapy in Exotics Supplement to Compendium on Continuing Education for the Practicing Veterinarian 20(3A): 34–48; 1998.

2. Carpenter, J.W., Mashima, T.Y., and Rupiper, D.J. Exotic animal formulary. Manhattan, KS: Greystone; 1996.

3. Ritchie, B.W., and Harrison, G.J. Formulary. In Ritchie, B.W., Harrison, G.J., and Harrison, L.R., eds., Avian medicine: Principles and application, pp. 457–478. Lake Worth, FL: Wingers Publishing; 1994.

4. Rosskopf, W.J., and Woerpel, R.W. Formulary of most commonly used medications in pet avian medicine. In Rosskopf, W.J., and Woerpel, R.W., eds., Diseases of cage and aviary birds, 3rd ed., pp. 1029–1040. Baltimore, MD: Williams and Wilkins; 1996.

5. Tully, T.N. Formulary. In Altman, R.B., Clubb, S.L., Dorrenstein, G.M., and Quesenberry, K., eds., Avian medicine and surgery, pp. 671–688. Philadelphia: W.B. Saunders; 1997.

6. Parrot, T. New clinical trials using acyclovir. In Proceedings of the Annual Conference of the Association of Avian Veterinarians, pp. 237–238. Phoenix, AZ; 1990.

7. Ritchie, B.W. Avian viruses: Function and control. Lake Worth, FL: Wingers Publishing; 1995.

8. Lumeij, J.T. Psittacine antimicrobial therapy. In Antimicrobial therapy in caged birds and exotic pets, pp. 38–48. Trenton, NJ: Veterinary Learning Systems; 1995.

9.   Orosz, S.E., Jones, M.P., Zagaya, N.K., and Frazier, D.L.
      Pharmacokinetic disposition of amoxicillin clavulanic acid in
      blue-fronted Amazon parrots. In Proceedings of the Annual
      Conference of the Association of Avian Veterinarians,
      pp. 17–23. St. Paul MN; 1998.

10.   Clubb, S.L. Special species: Birds. In Johnston, D.E., ed.,
      The Bristol veterinary handbook of antimicrobial therapy,
      2nd ed., pp. 188–199. Trenton, NJ: Veterinary Learning Sys-
      tems; 1987.

11.   Limoges, M.J. Plasma pharmacokinetics of orally adminis-
      tered azithromycin in mealy Amazon parrots. In Proceedings
      of the Annual Conference of the Association of Avian Veteri-
      narians, pp. 41–45. St. Paul, MN; 1998.

12.   Bauck, L., and Hoefer, H.L. Avian antimicrobial therapy. Sem
      Avian Exotic Pet Med 2:17–22; 1993.

13.   McDonald, S.E. Summary of medications for use in psitta-
      cine birds. J Assoc Avian Vet 3:120–127; 1989.

14.   Rupiper, D.J., and Ehrenberg, M. Introduction to pigeon prac-
      tice. In Proceedings of the Annual Conference of the Associa-
      tion of Avian Veterinarians, pp. 203–211. Reno, NV; 1994.

15.   Dorrestein, G.M. Avian chlamydiosis therapy. Sem Avian
      Exotic Pet Med 2:23–29; 1993.

16.   Powers, L., and Flammer, K. Dosing methods for administra-
      tion of doxycycline in cockatiels. In Proceedings of the
      Annual Conference of the Association of Avian Veterinarians,
      pp. 57–58. Reno, NV; 1997.

17.   Allen, D.G., et al., eds., Handbook of veterinary drugs,
      pp. 573–634. Philadelphia: J.B. Lippincott; 1993.

18. Murphy, J. Psittacine trichomoniasis. In Proceedings of the Annual Conference of the Association of Avian Veterinarians, pp. 21–24. New Orleans, LA; 1992.

19. St. Leger, J., and Shivaprasad, H.L. Passerine protozoal sinusitis. In Proceedings of the Annual Conference of the Association of Avian Veterinarians, pp. 121–124. St. Paul, MN; 1998.

20. Fudge, A.M. Avian giardiasis: Syndromes, diagnosis and therapy. In Proceedings of the Annual Conference of the Association of Avian Veterinarians, pp. 119–124. Miami, FL; 1986.

21. Clubb, S.L. Therapeutics. In Harrison, G.J., and Harrison, L.R., eds., Clinical avian medicine and surgery, pp. 327–355. Philadelphia: W.B. Saunders; 1986.

22. Bauck, L., Hillyer, E., and Hoefer, H. Rhinitis: Case reports. In Proceedings of the Annual Conference of the Association of Avian Veterinarians, pp. 134–139. New Orleans, LA; 1992.

23. Flammer, K. An overview of antifungal therapy in birds. In Proceedings of the Annual Conference of the Association of Avian Veterinarians, pp. 1–4. Nashville, TN; 1993.

24. Orosz, S.E., and Frazier, D.L. Antifungal agents: A review of their pharmacology and therapeutic indications. J Avian Med Surg 9:8–18; 1995.

25. Hines, R.S., Sharkey, P., and Friday, R.B. Itraconazole treatment of pulmonary, ocular and uropygial aspergillosis and candidiasis in birds. In Proceedings of the American Association of Zoo Veterinarians, pp. 322–326. Padre Island, TX; 1990.

26. Marshall, R. Avian anthelminthics and antiprotozoals. Sem Avian Exotic Pet Med 2:33–41; 1993.

27. Dorrestein, G.M. Diseases of passerines. In Proceedings of the Annual Conference of the Association of Avian Veterinarians, pp. 53–71. Boulder, CO; 1985.

28. Hogan, H.L., et al. Efficacy and safety of ivermectin treatment for scaley leg mite infestation in parakeets. In Proceedings of the American Association of Zoo Veterinarians, p. 156; 1984.

29. Clubb, S.L. Sarcocystis in psittacine birds. In Schubot, R.M., Clubb, K.J., and Clubb, S.L., eds., Psittacine aviculture, pp. 20–24. Loxahatchee, FL: Aviculture Breeding and Research Center; 1992.

30. Harlin, R.W. Pigeons. In Proceedings of the Annual Conference of the Association of Avian Veterinarians, pp. 361–373. Philadelphia, PA; 1995.

31. Ramsey, E.C. Trichomoniasis in a flock of budgerigars. In Proceedings of the Annual Conference of the Association of Avian Veterinarians, pp. 308–311. Phoenix, AZ; 1990.

32. Ramsey, E.C., and Grindlinger, H. Use of clomipramine in the treatment of obsessive behavior in psittacine birds. J Assoc Avian Vet 8:9; 1994.

33. Welle, K.R. A review of psychotropic drug therapy. In Proceedings of the Annual Conference of the Association of Avian Veterinarians, pp. 121–124. St. Paul, MN; 1998.

34. Turner, R. Trexan (naltrexone hydrochloride) use in feather picking in avian species. In Proceedings of the Annual Conference of the Association of Avian Veterinarians, pp. 116–118. Nashville, TN; 1993.

35. Gould, W.J. Caring for birds' skin and feathers. Vet Med (Jan.):53–63; 1995.

36. Swaim, S.F., and Gillette, R.L. An update on wound medications and dressings. Compendium on Continuing Education for the Practicing Veterinarian 20:1133–1143; 1998.

37. Wheler, C. Avian anesthetics, analgesics and tranquilizers. Sem Avian Exotic Pet Med 2:7–12; 1993.

38. Rupiper, D.J. Allopurinol in simple syrup for gout. J Assoc Avian Vet 7:219; 1993.

39. Taylor, M.T. Avian anesthesia: A clinical update. In Scientific Proceedings of the First International Conference of Zoo Avian Medicine, pp. 519–524. Oahu, HI; 1987.

40. LaBonde, J. Household poisonings in caged birds. In Kirk, R.W., ed., Current veterinary therapy XII, Small animal practice, pp. 1299–1303. Philadelphia: W.B. Saunders; 1995.

41. LaBonde, J. Toxicity in pet avian patients. Sem Avian Exotic Pet Med 4:23–31; 1995.

42. Bauck, L. Analgesics in avian medicine. In Proceedings of the Annual Conference of the Association of Avian Veterinarians, pp. 239–244. Phoenix, AZ; 1990.

43. Hoefer, H.L. Hepatic fibrosis and colchicine therapy. J Assoc Avian Vet 5:193; 1991.

44. Cornelissen, H., Ducatelle, R., and Roels, S. Successful treatment of a channel-billed toucan *(Ramphastos vitellinus)* with iron storage disease by chelation therapy: Sequential monitoring of the iron content of the liver during the treatment period by quantitative chemical and image analyses. J Avian Med Surg 9:131–137; 1995.

45.   Bauck, L. A practitioner's guide to avian medicine. Lake-
      wood, CO: American Animal Hospital Assoc.; 1993.

46.   Ritchie, B.W. Emergency care of avian patients. In North
      American Veterinary Conference Proceedings, Vol. 8,
      pp. 806–808; 1994.

47.   Van Sant, F. Zinc and parrots. In Proceedings of the Annual
      Conference of the Association of Avian Veterinarians,
      pp. 305–312. St. Paul, MN; 1998.

48.   McDonald, S.E. Summary of medications for use in psitta-
      cine birds. In Association of Avian Veterinarians Introduction
      to Avian Medicine and Surgery Basics Core Manual, Pro-
      ceedings of the Annual Conference of the Association of
      Avian Veterinarians, pp. T3-1 to T3-12. Chicago, IL; 1991.

49.   Lightfoot, T.L. How I approach chronic egg laying. In North
      American Veterinary Conference Proceedings, Vol. 12, p. 757;
      1998.

50.   Rae, M. Endocrine disease in pet birds. Sem Avian Exotic Pet
      Med 4:32–38; 1995.

51.   Rosskopf, W.J., and Woerpel, R.W. Avian obstetrical medicine.
      In Proceedings of the Annual Conference of the Association
      of Avian Veterinarians, pp. 323–336. Nashville, TN; 1993.

52.   Oglesbee, B.L., McDonald, S.E., and Warthen, K. Avian
      digestive system disorders. In Birchard, S.J., and Sherding,
      R.G., eds., Saunders manual of small animal practice,
      pp. 1290–1301. Philadelphia: W.B. Saunders; 1994.

53.   Huff, D.G. Avian fluid therapy and nutritional therapeutics.
      Sem Avian Exotic Pet Med 2:13–16; 1993.

Ferret Drug Dosages
Susan A. Brown, DVM

General Guidelines

Although the number of chemical agents used in the treatment of ferret patients has increased dramatically in the past 10 years, the overwhelming majority of the dosages for these agents have been derived from empirical use. Few pharmacokinetic studies have been conducted on drugs used for treating ferrets, with the notable exception of some anesthetics and analgesics. Therefore, the ferret drug dosage chart that follows these guidelines is not divided into pharmacokinetic and nonpharmacokinetic studies. General references are provided for most of the drugs, and anyone who seeks more information is encouraged to consult these sources. In addition, an asterisk is used to indicate agents personally used by the author with ferrets; these listings are accompanied by pertinent comments based on anecdotal experiences.

Since there are no USDA approved drugs for ferrets (except for rabies and canine distemper vaccines), the question arises as to whether it is advisable to obtain a consent form from the owner when treating ferrets. The decision must be based on the legal requirements of the locality or of the veterinary profession in the future, on the owner being dealt with, and on the risk factors of the drug being used. No drugs are included in this formulary that are considered dangerous to ferrets, and cautionary comments are provided for drugs that have some risk but are still considered beneficial. However, because risk does exist for those drugs, it falls on the practitioner to shoulder the responsibility for using these agents with ferret patients.

43

The practitioner must always be alert for possible drug reactions or side effects.

The general guidelines for drug use in ferrets are no different from those for drug use in the canine or feline patient. The least number of agents possible should be used to accomplish treatment goals. Drugs should be used responsibly based on clinical judgment and diagnostic testing. Ferrets deserve as high a quality of care as canine and feline patients. Antibiotics are probably the most overused of all drugs in ferrets (as well as in other species) and should be used only when appropriate and not automatically whenever an ill ferret is presented. Corticosteroids are invaluable for treating a number of common diseases in the ferret, such as insulinoma, lymphoma (alone or as part of the chemotherapy protocol), eosinophilic gastroenteritis, and severe gastritis, to name a few. However, they are often used at a much higher dose than is necessary. Whenever a ferret has to be placed on lifelong corticosteroid therapy, it is important to start at the lowest possible dose and work up slowly to accomplish the treatment goals. Starting at a high dose makes it difficult to reduce the dose later in the treatment period and may lead to iatrogenic hyperadrenocorticoidism. In ferrets, there is generally more consistent control of clinical signs with a twice daily dose of corticosteroids at a lower per dose amount than with a once daily dose at a higher amount.

Because ferrets are such small patients, most weighing 1 kg or less, it is invaluable to use a compounding pharmacy to formulate liquid medications out of tablets or injectables that are more palatable and easier to dose. There are numerous pharmacies devoted to veterinary drug compounding across the country, many of which have standard formulations for a number of drugs for ferrets. Most ferrets readily take medications hidden in sweet or oily substances. The practitioner must be cautious, however, when using sweet medications, because ferrets are prone to developing insulinoma and the sugar content of the medication could potentially cause problems with treatment. It is important to avoid refined sugar if possible and to use only tiny amounts of natural sweeteners (fruit juice, honey, etc.). Oils are preferable if the drug can be put into that form because the fat not only is tasty but is metabolized more readily and safely than sugars. Medications can also be mixed on a per dose basis with strained meat, human baby food, or feline canned food products.

Drug Dosages for Ferrets

ANTIBACTERIAL AGENTS

DRUG DOSE AND ROUTE	COMMENTS
Amikacin[1]	
8–16 mg/kg total per day, divided q 8–24h SC, IM, IV	If given IV, amikacin should be diluted with saline at 4 ml/kg and administered over 20 minutes to avoid neuromuscular blockade and renal failure.
Amoxicillin[1,2,*]	
10–25 mg/kg q 12–24h PO, SC	May be used in combination with metronidazole and bismuth subsalicylate or with only clarithromycin in the treatment of *Helicobacter mustelae* gastritis. Good broad-spectrum agent for gastrointestinal and respiratory infections.
Amoxicillin 25 mg/ml + clavulanate potassium 6.25 mg/ml[3]	
12.5 mg/kg q 12h PO	
Ampicillin[4,*]	
5–30 mg/kg q 12h SC, IM, IV	
Cefadroxil*	
15–20 mg/kg q 12h PO	Broad-spectrum agent.

IM = intramuscularly
IV = intravenously
IT = intratracheally
PO = per os; orally
SC = subcutaneously

Note: Asterisks indicate agents the author has used personally with ferrets. These listings are accompanied by pertinent comments based on anecdotal experiences.

Cephalexin[1,]*
15–25 mg/kg *q* 12h PO

Broad-spectrum agent for respiratory and urinary infections.

Cephaloridine[4,]*
10–15 mg/kg *q* 24h SC, IM

Broad-spectrum agent.

Chloramphenicol[1,2,3,]*
50 mg/kg *q* 12h PO (palmitate)
30–50 mg/kg *q* 12h SC, IM, IV (succinate)

Chloramphenicol palmitate may be unavailable in some areas. Chloramphenicol is the treatment of choice for proliferative bowel disease. Use for minimum of 14 days. Advise owner of potential human toxicities from contact.

Ciprofloxacin[1,2,3,]*
5–15 mg/kg *q* 12h PO or
10–30 mg/kg *q* 24h PO

Used in the same situations as enrofloxacin.

Ciprofloxacin hydrochloride 0.3% ophthalmic[3]
2–3 drops *q* 12h topically

Clarithromycin*
50 mg/kg *q* 12–24h PO

Use in combination with amoxicillin or metronidazole plus bismuth subsalicylate for the treatment of *Helicobacter mustelae* gastritis.

Clindamycin hydrochloride[3,]*
5.5–10 mg/kg *q* 12h PO

For anaerobic infections. Good for bone and dental disease.

Cloxacillin[1,2,3]
10 mg/kg *q* 6h PO, IM, IV

continued

Enrofloxacin[1,3],*
5–10 mg/kg *q* 12h PO, SC, IM, or 10–20 mg/kg *q* 24h PO, SC, IM

Broad-spectrum agent; however, this drug has been overused and antibiotic resistance may ultimately be the result in the future. May use IM for a few days, but sterile abscesses may result. Oral administration is preferred. Injectable form may be mixed with a palatable syrup.

Erythromycin[1,2,3]
10–15 mg/kg *q* 6h PO

Gentamicin[1,2,3]
4–8 mg/kg total per day, divided *q* 8–24h SC, IM, IV

If given IV, gentamicin should be diluted with saline at 4 ml/kg and administered over 20 minutes to avoid neuromuscular blockade and renal failure.

Lincomycin[1,2]
10–15 mg/kg *q* 8h PO or 10 mg/kg *q* 12h IM

Metronidazole[1],*
10–25 mg/kg *q* 12h PO

For anaerobic infections. May be used along with amoxicillin or clarithromycin in the treatment of *Helicobacter mustelae* gastritis. May be used along with chloramphenicol for proliferative colitis.

Neomycin[1,2,3]
10–20 mg/kg *q* 6–12h PO

Netilmicin[1]
6–8 mg/kg *q* 24h SC, IM, IV

If given IV, netilmicin should be diluted with saline at 4 ml/kg and administered over 20 minutes to avoid neuromuscular blockade and renal failure.

Oxytetracycline[1,2]
20 mg/kg *q* 8h PO

Penicillin G (sodium or potassium)[1,2,*]
40,000 IU/kg *q* 24h IM or
  20,000 IU/kg *q* 12h IM

Sulfadimethoxine[1,3,*]
25 mg/kg *q* 24h PO, SC, IM

Sulfasoxazole[3]
50 mg/kg *q* 8h PO

Tetracycline[1,3]
25 mg/kg *q* 8–12h PO

Trimethoprim–sulfa combinations[1,3,4,*]
15–30 mg/kg *q* 12h PO, SC   Dose is based on the mg amount of *combined* drugs.

Tylosin[1,2,*]
10 mg/kg *q* 12–24h PO

ANTIPARASITIC AGENTS	
DRUG DOSE AND ROUTE	COMMENTS

Amitraz[1]

  Apply to affected skin 3–6 times at 14-day intervals.

Amprolium[4]
19 mg/kg *q* 24h PO

Carbaryl[1,*]
0.5% shampoo or 5% powder   Treat once a week for 3–6 weeks.

continued

Decoquinate[4]

0.5 mg/kg *q* 24h PO   Mix in moist food.

Diethylcarbamazine[2,3]

2.75–11 mg/kg *q* 24h PO   Heartworm preventative; ivermectin is preferred.

Imidacloprid*

0.4 ml/ferret of 9.1% solution   For flea control. Appears to be safe.
  q 30d topically

Ivermectin[1,2,]*

0.006 mg/kg *q* 30d PO   For heartworm prevention. Can use canine
                  products.

0.5 mg/kg PO, SC   Heartworm microfilaricide; 3–4 week post-
                  adulticide treatment.

0.50–1.0 mg/kg PO, SC   Use at this dosage range for sarcoptic mange.
                  Repeat at 2-week intervals for at least three
                  doses.
                  For *Otodectes* infestation use 1.0 mg/kg dose,
                  putting one half of the total dose in each ear;
                  repeat in 2 weeks.

Lime sulfur[1]

                  Dilute 1:40 in water; wash ferret with solution
                  once a week for 6 weeks.

Luferon*

30 mg/kg *q* 30d PO   For flea control. Appears to be safe in ferrets.

Metronidazole

20 mg/kg *q* 12–24h PO[1,3,]* or   For gastrointestinal protozoal infections. Use for
35 mg/kg *q* 24h PO[2,]*   5 to 10 days.

Milbemycin oxime[1,3,]*

1.15–2.33 mg/kg *q* 30d PO   Use for heartworm prevention. Use smallest
                  dose canine tablets.

Piperazine[1,3]

50–100 mg/kg *q* 14d PO   Use at least two doses.

Praziquantel[1,2,*]
5–12.5 mg/ferret PO, SC;   Use for cestodes.
  repeat in 14 days

Pyrantel pamoate[2,3]
4.4 mg/kg PO; repeat in
  14 days

Pyrethrin products[1,*]
                       Use topically as directed once per week as
                       needed.

Sulfadimethoxine[1,*]
50 mg/kg PO once; then   For coccidial infections.
  25 mg/kg *q* 24h for 9 days PO

ANTIFUNGAL AGENTS	
DRUG DOSE AND ROUTE	COMMENTS
Amphotericin B[1,3]	
0.4–0.8 mg/kg *q* 7d IV	Total dose not to exceed 25 mg, or follow published canine protocols.
Griseofulvin[1,3]	
25 mg/kg *q* 24h PO	Follow feline protocols.
Ketoconazole[1,2,3]	
10–50 mg/kg *q* 12–24h PO	Not effective for controlling signs of adrenal disease.

ANESTHETIC AND ANALGESIC AGENTS	
DRUG DOSE AND ROUTE	COMMENTS
Acepromazine[2,3,*]	
0.1–0.25 mg/kg SC, IM	Preanesthetic; light sedation
0.2–0.5 mg/kg SC, IM	Tranquilization; the lower end of this dose may be used with 25–35 mg/kg of ketamine for short-term anesthesia.

continued

Aspirin[3,*]
0.5–20 mg/kg *q* 8–24h PO

Atipamezole[5,*]
0.4 mg/kg IM   Reversal agent for medetomidine. This dose is used to reverse 0.08 mg/kg medetomidine. Normal calculation is same *volume* (not mg dose) of atipamezole used as volume of medetomidine used.

Atropine sulfate[3,4,6,*]
0.04–0.05 mg/kg SC, IM, IV   Preanesthetic.

Buprenorphine[1,2,*]
0.01–0.03 mg/kg *q* 8–12h SC, IM, IV   Analgesic.

Butorphanol tartrate[1,2,5,*]
0.05–0.5 mg/kg *q* 8–12h SC, IM   Analgesic; can be used pre-, intra-, or postoperatively.
0.1 mg/kg SC, IM   Use at this dose in combination with ketamine (5 mg/kg IM) and medetomidine (0.08 mg/kg IM) for anesthesia with analgesia.

Carprofen[*]
1 mg/kg *q* 12–24h PO   Nonsteroidal antiinflammatory drug (NSAID) with fewer gastrointestinal effects than flunixin. Use with caution in ferrets with enteritis or gastritis. Do not use in conjunction with corticosteroids.

Diazepam[1,2,3,4,*]
1–2 mg/kg PO, SC, IM, IV, as needed   For seizure control and sedation.
1.0–1.5 mg/kg/h continuous IV   For control of status epilepticus.

Fentanyl/droperidol[4,7]
0.15 ml/kg IM   For minor surgical procedures and deep sedation.

Flunixin meglumine[1,6,]*
0.5–2.0 mg/kg *q* 12–24h PO,
IM, IV

NSAID. Use with caution in ferrets with enteritis or gastritis. Do not use in conjunction with corticosteroids. Be cautious using it for more than 5 days continuously as possibility of gastrointestinal ulcers exists. Injectable form can be administered orally in a palatable syrup.

Glycopyrrolate[6]
0.01 mg/kg IM

Preanesthetic.

Ketamine[2,3,4,6,7,]*

May require premedication with atropine due to hypersalivation.

10–20 mg/kg IM
Tranquilization.

25–40 mg/kg IM
Anesthetic dose; however, best if used in combination with an analgesic.

Ketamine + acepromazine[2,3,]*
20–40 mg/kg ketamine IM +
0.2–0.35 mg/kg
acepromazine SC, IM

Anesthesia.

Ketamine + diazepam[2,3,4,]*
25–35 mg/kg ketamine IM +
2–3 mg/kg diazepam IM

Anesthesia.

Ketoprofen*
1 mg/kg *q* 24h PO, IM

NSAID. Same cautions as listed for flunixin meglumine.

Medetomidine[5,]*
0.08 mg/kg IM

Sedative for noninvasive procedures. Reverse with atipamezole at 0.40 mg/kg IM.

continued

Medetomidine + ketamine + butorphanol[5,*]

0.08 mg/kg medetomidine IM + 5 mg/kg ketamine IM + 0.10 mg/kg butorphanol IM

Anesthesia for short surgical procedures. All three drugs are given at the same time and may be combined in the same syringe. Reverse with atipamezole at 0.40 mg/kg IM.

Meperidine[1,6]

5–20 mg/kg q 2–4h SC, IM, IV   Analgesic.

Morphine[6]

0.5–5.0 mg/kg q 2–6h SC, IM   Analgesic.

Nalbuphine[6]

0.5–1.5 mg/kg q 2–3h IM, IV   Analgesic.

Oxymorphone[1,6]

0.05–0.20 mg/kg q 8–12h SC, IM, IV   Analgesic.

Pentazocine[1,6]

5–10 mg/kg q 4h IM   Analgesic.

Phenobarbitol elixir[1,*]

1–2 mg/kg q 8–12h PO   For seizure control. Titrate dose for maintenance.

Tiletamine-zolazepam[6,8]

12–22 mg/kg IM   Sedation at lower dose; use higher dose for minor surgical procedures.

MISCELLANEOUS AGENTS

DRUG DOSE AND ROUTE	COMMENTS

Amantadine

6 mg/kg q 12h PO   Antiviral agent. May be useful in the treatment of influenza in ferrets.

Aminophylline[1,*]

4 mg/kg q 12h PO, IM, IV   Bronchodilation.

Atenolol[9]

6.25 mg/ferret *q* 24h PO   Beta-adrenergic blocker used in hypertrophic
cardiomyopathy.

Atropine sulfate[1,3]

5–10 mg/kg SC, IM   For organophosphate toxicity. See anesthetic
section for dose as preanesthetic.

Barium (20%)*

15 mg/kg PO   Used for gastrointestinal contrast study.

Bismuth subsalicylate[1,]*

0.25 mg/kg *q* 8–12h PO   Use in conjunction with other drugs for
treatment of gastric ulcers. Ferrets object to
its taste, so it may have to be mixed with a
palatable syrup.

Captopril[2]

1.6 mg/kg (1/8 of tablet) *q* 48h Vasodilator. This is the starting dose. Eventually
PO   increase frequency to *q* 12–24h. Can cause
lethargy.

Chlorpheniramine*

1–2 mg/kg *q* 8–12h PO   Antihistamine for control of sneezing and
coughing.

Cimetidine[1,2,]*

5–10 mg/kg *q* 8h PO, SC, IM, Inhibits gastric acid secretion. Used for
IV   treatment of gastric ulcers. Unpalatable;
should be mixed with a palatable syrup. Give
IV bolus slowly.

Cisapride[1,3]

0.5 mg/kg *q* 8h PO   Gastrointestinal motility stimulant.

Dexamethasone*

0.5–2.0 mg/kg PO, SC, IM, IV

continued

Dexamethasone sodium phosphate[1],*

4–8 mg/kg IM, IV, once   Use for initial shock therapy.

Diazoxide[1,2],*

5–30 mg/kg *q* 12h PO   Insulin-blocking agent used in the treatment of insulinoma. Start at the low end of the dose and gradually work up to effective dose. Usually used in conjunction with corticosteroids. May cause hypertension, lethargy, depression, and/or nausea.

Digoxin elixir[1,2,3],*

0.005–0.01 mg/kg *q* 12–24h PO for maintenance   Positive inotrope for dilated cardiomyopathy. Start with higher dose to load for the first 24–48 hours, then reduce. Monitor blood digoxin concentration if possible.

Diltiazem[1,9]

1.5–7.5 mg/kg *q* 12h PO   Calcium channel blocker used for hypertrophic cardiomyopathy. Adjust dose as needed.

Diphenhydramine[1],*

0.5–2 mg/kg *q* 8–12h PO, IM   Antihistamine used to control sneezing and coughing. Useful in treating anaphylactic reactions to vaccination. May be used prevaccination in cases where previous anaphylaxis occurred. However, note that this pretreatment may not be 100% effective.

Doxapram[1,2,3,7]

1–11 mg/kg IV   Respiratory stimulant.

Enalapril[1,3,9],*

0.25–0.5 mg/kg *q* 24–48h PO   Vasodilator for dilated cardiomyopathy. Well tolerated. Monitor for weakness and anorexia. Use with caution when renal disease is present.

Enteral feeding[3]

200–300 kcal/day — This is maintenance level. Best to give assist feedings in 4–6 small meals a day.

Epinephrine

20 mcg/kg SC, IM, IV, IT — Used for treating anaphylactic reactions.

Epoetin alpha*

50–150 IU/kg *q* 48h PO, IM

50–150 IU/kg *q* 7d PO, IM, for maintenance

Useful in stimulating red blood cell production (chemotherapy, renal disease, etc.). Use *q* 48h until desired pack cell volume is reached and then use maintenance dose.

Famotidine*

0.25–0.50 mg/kg *q* 24h PO, IV — Inhibits gastric acid secretion. Used in gastric ulcer therapy.

Filigrastim*

5 mg/kg *q* 24h SC — A human granulocyte colony stimulating factor. Used in chemotherapy.

Fluid therapy[3],*

60–75 ml/kg *q* 24h PO, SC, IV — This is maintenance fluid level. Be sure to correct for dehydration.

Flurbiprofen sodium[3]

1–2 drops *q* 12–24h topically — Topical NSAID for ophthalmic inflammation.

Flutamide[10]

10 mg/kg *q* 12h PO — Antiandrogenic drug used to alleviate the signs of adrenal neoplasia or hyperplasia. Most useful for reducing enlarged periurethral prostate tissue. Lifetime treatment. Tablets can be made into a pleasant tasting suspension.

Furosemide[9],*

1–4 mg/kg *q* 8–12h PO, SC, IM, IV

Diuretic. First drug commonly used in treating cardiac disease.

continued

GnRH[2,*]

20 mcg/ferret once, IM — Used to terminate estrus. Give after ferret has been in estrus for a minimum of 10 days. Repeat in 14 days if no response. Perform complete blood cell count to detect anemia if ferret has been in estrus 21 days or longer.

hCG[1,2,3,*]

100 IU/ferret once, IM — Used to terminate estrus. Same directions apply as for GnRH.

Hydrocortisone sodium succinate[2,3]

25–40 mg/kg IV — For shock therapy.

Hydroxyzine hydrochloride[1]

2 mg/kg *q* 8h PO — Used for management of some types of pruritus. Because it acts as a mild sedative, it should be used with great caution with central nervous system depressant drugs. May cause drowsiness.

Insulin, NPH[2,*]

0.5–6.0 IU/kg *q* 12–24h or to effect, SC — Used for treatment of diabetes mellitus and other hyperglycemic conditions (e.g., glucagonoma or postsurgically after insulinoma removal). Follow similar guidelines as for the feline patient. Other forms of insulin may be tried. Oral hypoglycemics do not appear to be effective in ferrets.

Iron dextran[1,3]

10 mg/ferret IM

Kaolin/pectin[1,*]

1–2 ml/kg *q* 2–6h as needed, PO — Gastrointestinal coating agent.

Lactulose syrup[1,]*

1.5–3 mg/kg *q* 12h PO — Absorbs blood ammonia (as in hepatic disease). May cause soft stools at higher dose due to its laxative effect.

Loperamide*

0.2 mg/kg *q* 12h PO — Antidiarrheal. Useful in the treatment of epizootic catarrhal gastroenteritis (ECE).

Melarsamine hydrochloride

2.5 mg/kg IM once, followed 1 month later by two doses IM 24 hours apart — Used for treatment of heartworm disease.

Metoclopramide[1]

0.2–1 mg/kg *q* 6–8h PO, SC — Gastrointestinal motility stimulant.

Mitotane (o,p'-DDD)*

50 mg/ferret *q* 24h for 7 days; then *q* 48h until signs resolved; then *q* 7d or as needed — Chemotherapy drug specific for adrenal tissue. Used to treat adrenocortical neoplasia or hyperplasia. Drug should be placed into small gelatin capsules by a pharmacist. Results are variable; drug may alleviate signs for a period of time but rarely results in a cure.

Nitroglycerine 2% ointment[2,3]

1/16–1/8 inch/ferret *q* 12–24h topically on shaved inner thigh or pinna — Vasodilator for cardiomyopathy.

Oxytocin[1,2,]*

0.2–10 USP units/kg SC, IM — Expels retained fetus and stimulates lactation.

continued

59

Prednisone, prednisolone[1,2,3,*]

0.10–2.5 mg/kg *q* 12–24h PO   Corticosteroid with multiple uses (chemotherapy, insulinoma, eosinophilic gastroenteritis, etc.). When treating early insulinoma, start with lowest dose *q* 12h and increase as needed to control signs.

Prochlorperazine[3]

0.13 mg/kg *q* 3–4h deep IM   For control of nausea and vomiting.

Proligestone[1]

50 mg/kg once, IM   Use before onset of female reproductive season.

Propanolol[1,2,*]

0.50–2.0 mg/kg *q* 12–24h PO, SC   Beta blocker and vasodilator used in hypertrophic cardiomyopathy. May cause lethargy and anorexia.

Prostaglandin F[2 alpha]

0.1–0.5 mg/ferret as needed, IM   Used in metritis to help expel necrotic debris.

Stanozolol[1,3,*]

0.5 mg/kg *q* 24h PO, SC, IM, or 10–25 mg/kg *q* 7d PO, SC, IM   Anabolic steroid.

Sucralfate[1,3,*]

25 mg/kg up to 125 mg/ferret *q* 6–8h PO   Used in treatment of gastrointestinal ulcers. Do not use with cimetidine or other antacids as sucralfate is active only in an acid environmnent.

Sulfasalazine[1]

10–20 mg/kg *q* 12h PO   Used in treatment of ulcerative enteritis or colitis.

Theophylline elixir[1,3,*]

4.25 mg/kg *q* 8–12h PO   Bronchodilator.

Vitamin B complex[1,*]

1–2 mg/kg as needed, IM   Dose listed is based on thiamine content.

References

1. Smith, D.A., and Burgman, P.M. Formulary. In Hillyer, E.V., and Quesenberry, K.E., eds., Ferrets, rabbits and rodents: Clinical medicine and surgery, pp. 394–397. Philadelphia: W.B. Saunders; 1997.

2. Carpenter, J.W., Mashima, T.Y., and Rupiper, D.J. Exotic animal formulary. Manhattan, KS: Greystone; 1996.

3. Johnson-Delaney, C.A. Exotic companion medicine handbook. Lake Worth, FL: Wingers Publishing.

4. Hawk, D.F., and Leary, S.L. Formulary for laboratory animals. Ames: Iowa State Press; 1995.

5. Ko, J.C.H., Heaton-Jones, T.G., and Nicklin, C.F. Evaluation of the sedative and cardiorespiratory effects of medetomidine, medetomidine-butorphanol, medetomidine-ketamine and medetomidine-butorphanol-ketamine in ferrets. JAAHA 33:438–448; 1997.

6. Heard, D.J. Principles and techniques of anesthesia and analgesia for exotic practice. Vet Clin North Am/Small Anim Pract 23:1301–1327; 1993.

7. Flecknell, P.A. Laboratory animal anesthesia. London: Academic Press; 1987.

8. Payton, A.J., and Pick, J.R. Evaluation of a combination of tiletamine and zolazepam as an anesthetic for ferrets. Lab Anim Sci 39:243–246; 1989.

9. Stamoulis, M.E. Cardiac disease in ferrets. Sem Avian Exotic Pet Med 4:43–48, 1995.

10. Rosenthal, K.R. Personal communication; 1997.

Rabbit Drug Dosages
Natalie Antinoff, DVM, Diplomate ABVP (Avian Practice)

General Guidelines

This formulary is intended to provide the reader with a comprehensive listing of the drugs and dosages most commonly used in rabbits. Few pharmacokinetic studies have been conducted on these drugs. Dosages derived from such studies are indicated by asterisks within the formulary. The majority of the drugs and dosages in this formulary are based on empirical studies or clinical experience; although references are provided, the reader should note that these dosages are not based on pharmacologic studies.

Because rabbits are frequently used for drug studies in human medicine, there is a tendency to try to interpret the results for use in rabbits. In some of these studies, certain dosages have been deemed safe, and the results *may* be useful in clinical situations. However, many of these studies have investigated LD50 and/or safety rather than efficacy. Extreme discretion is recommended when interpreting the results of these investigational drug studies for use in rabbits.

The following basic guidelines should prove useful to practitioners:

    1.   Antibiotics should be used only when bacterial infection is suspected based on the clinical presentation of the rabbit. The random use of antibacterial agents "prophylactically" leads to increased antibiotic resistance and decreased efficacy when infection is present. Antibiotics can also adversely affect gastrointestinal (particularly cecal) bacterial flora and may lead to diarrhea, gastric stasis, and enterotoxemia.

2.   Antimicrobial choice should be based on culture and sensitivity whenever possible. Abscesses in rabbits typically are caseous rather than liquid, and the centers are often necrotic. Simply swabbing the center of the abscess is inadequate for microbial sampling. When obtaining samples for culture from an abscess, the practitioner should include a piece of the capsule of the abscess to increase the bacterial yield. Samples may be submitted in standard culture transport media or may be collected in sterile saline if plating is done within 24–36 hours.

3.   Several antibacterial drugs have been implicated in fatal enterotoxemia in rabbits, including penicillin and its derivatives (amoxicillin, ampicillin), erythromycin, lincomycin, tetracyclines, and cephalosporins. Use of these drugs should be avoided in rabbits. If antibiotic-induced enterotoxemia is suspected, treatment should include fluid administration, oral cholestyramine, and increased dietary fiber. (Injectable procaine or benzathine penicillin may be used in very limited and specific situations, such as treponema.)

4.   Bactericidal antibiotics should be selected over bacteriostatic antibiotics when possible. Combining a bactericidal and a bacteriostatic antibiotic will inhibit the efficacy of the bactericidal drug, which depends on replicating bacteria.

5.   Anaerobic organisms may be present, particularly in abscesses. However, many drugs that are effective against anaerobic organisms are contraindicated in rabbits and should be avoided. Metronidazole can be used with minimal adverse effects in most rabbit patients.

Additional Guidelines for Specific Drug Categories

Antimicrobial Agents

Aminoglycosides have a predominantly gram-negative spectrum, with very limited efficacy against gram-positive and anaerobic organisms. Further, their efficacy decreases in conditions of low oxygen or in the presence of exudates. Severe and potentially irreversible side effects from aminoglycoside use include nephrotoxicity and ototoxicity.[1] Recent studies have demonstrated a decreased potential for nephrotoxicity when aminoglycosides are administered at high doses every 24 hours (rather than at lower doses more frequently), with no decrease in efficacy.[2-4] Blood urea nitrogen and creatinine should be monitored if aminoglycoside therapy is selected. The use of loop diuretics or cephalosporins with aminoglycosides should be avoided due to the increased potential for nephrotoxicity and ototoxicity. Synergistic interactions occur with trimethoprim-sulfa, metronidazole, and fluoroquinolones.

Cephalosporins are typically not recommended for use in rabbits because of the potential for enterotoxemia. Although third-generation cephalosporins may be safer than first- or second-generation cephalosporins, their use is often limited by cost constraints.

Chloramphenicol is a broad-spectrum bacteriostatic drug with good efficacy against gram-positive, gram-negative, and anaerobic organisms. It penetrates the respiratory tract, reproductive tract, and central nervous system if the blood-brain barrier is violated. The oral suspension, chloramphenicol palmitate, is no longer commercially available but can be obtained through compounding pharmacies. Because idiosyncratic bone marrow suppression may occur in humans from the handling of this drug, it is recommended that gloves be distributed to clients when chloramphenicol is prescribed.

Fluoroquinolones are effective against gram-negative bacteria and limited gram-positive organisms. Although there is limited bacterial resistance to these drugs, inappropriate use is leading to more resistance in specific clinical patients. Fluoroquinolones are well tolerated in rabbits, even at high doses. Ciprofloxacin tablets can be compounded into oral suspension. Note that injectable enrofloxacin can cause severe skin and muscle necrosis in rabbits and is not recommended for more than a single dose. Enrofloxacin's spectrum can be extended when it is combined with metronidazole or third-generation cephalosporins. The author has seen two rabbits who presented with neurologic signs after long-term (>6 month) use of enrofloxacin at high doses. In both rabbits, the signs were resolved when the drug was discontinued.

Penicillins are contraindicated for oral use in rabbits. However, for treponema cuniculi (rabbit syphilis) or specific bacterial infections, injectable procaine or benzathine penicillin may be required. Increasing dietary fiber consumption may reduce the potential for enterotoxemia in these cases, although some risk will still exist.

Sulfonamides are bacteriostatic when used alone but bactericidal when used in combination with trimethoprim. The combination is effective against gram-positive and gram-negative organisms and distributes well to the respiratory, alimentary, reproductive, and urinary tracts as well as to the skin and central nervous system. Side effects that are commonly seen in dogs have not been reported in rabbits.

Tetracyclines have been shown to have limited efficacy against pasteurellosis; therapeutic levels are not achieved when tetracyclines are dosed in drinking water.[5]

Miscellaneous Agents

The use of steroids should be avoided in rabbits unless absolutely necessary. Rabbits are highly susceptible to the adverse effects of steroid use. Subclinical pasteurellosis, which is present in many rabbits, can become significant when rabbits are immunosuppressed. Steroids may also lead to gastric ulceration. Because topical steroids can be systemically absorbed, they should also be avoided. When indicated, steroid therapy should be limited and quickly tapered, and the patient should be monitored closely.

Gastric motility stimulating agents such as metoclopramide and cisapride should be avoided if there is any suspicion of intestinal obstruction. Agents that limit or decrease gastric motility should be avoided in all rabbit patients.

Drug Dosages for Rabbits

ANTIBACTERIAL AGENTS

DRUG DOSE AND ROUTE	COMMENTS

Amikacin sulfate[2–4,6]

6–10 mg/kg q 24h SC, IM, IV — May cause nephrotoxicity; decreased nephrotoxicity has been shown to occur when drug is administered at higher doses every 24 hours than at the lower doses published previously. Dilute and administer as a slow bolus for IV use.

Cephalexin[7]

11–22 mg/kg q 8h PO — Use with caution; may cause enterotoxemia.

Cephalothin sodium[7]

12.5 mg/kg q 6h IM — Use with caution; may cause enterotoxemia.

Chloramphenicol palmitate[7–10]

30–50 mg/kg q 12h PO — Available through compounding pharmacies.

Chloramphenicol sodium succinate[7–10]

30–50 mg/kg q 8–12h SC, IM, IV

Chlortetracycline[6,11,12]

50 mg/kg q 12–24h PO

IM = intramuscularly
IP = intraperitoneally
IV = intravenously
PO = per os; orally
SC = subcutaneously

Note: Asterisks indicate dosages derived from pharmacokinetic studies.

Ciprofloxacin[6,7,9]
5–20 mg/kg q 12–24h PO

May have improved efficacy if administered at higher doses every 24 hours than at the lower dosages published previously.

Doxycycline[6,8]
2.5–5 mg/kg q 12h PO

Enrofloxacin[6–10,12–15]
5–20 mg/kg q 12–24h PO, SC, IM, IV*

Dilute and administer slowly for IV use. For all routes of administration, may have improved efficacy if administered at higher doses every 24 hours than at the lower dosages published previously. May lead to muscle necrosis with repeated IM or SC use.

Gentamicin sulfate[2–4,6]*
5–8 mg/kg q 24h SC, IM, IV*

May cause nephrotoxicity; decreased nephrotoxicity if administered at higher doses every 24 hours than at the lower dosages published previously. Dilute and administer as a slow bolus for IV use.

Metronidazole[6,9,12]
20 mg/kg q 12h PO, IV

Minocycline[16]
6 mg/kg q 8h PO, IV*

Neomycin[17]
30 mg/kg q 12h PO

Netilmicin[6]
6–8 mg/kg q 24h SC, IM, IV

Oxytetracycline[18]
15 mg/kg q 8h SC, IM*

Diarrhea and anorexia may occur at higher doses.

continued

**Penicillin G
(procaine, benzathine)**[6,9,12]
42,000–60,000 IU/kg *q* 48h   For specific bacterial infection when indicated.
  SC, IM
42,000–60,000 IU/kg *q* 7 days For treatment of rabbit syphilis.
  SC, IM

Sulfamethazine[6,15]
1–5 mg/ml drinking water

Sulfaquinoxaline[11]
1,000 mg/L drinking water   May have some efficacy against *Bordatella* spp.

Tetracycline[6,11]
50 mg/kg *q* 8h PO   Not effective against pasteurellosis in clinical
                trials.

Trimethoprim-sulfa[6–11]
30 mg/kg *q* 12h PO, SC, IM

Tylosin[6,11,12,17]
10 mg/kg *q* 12h PO, SC, IM

ANTIFUNGAL AGENTS

DRUG DOSE AND ROUTE   COMMENTS

Griseofulvin[6–9,15]
12.5 mg/kg *q* 12h PO or   Treat for 4–6 weeks.
  25 mg/kg *q* 24h PO

Lime sulfur dip (2.5–3%)[6,7,15]

                Saturate coat every 5 to 7 days for 4–6 weeks;
                  protect rabbit's eyes.

Nystatin[12]
3–5 ml *q* 12–24h PO

ANTIPARASITIC AGENTS

DRUG DOSE AND ROUTE	COMMENTS

Amprolium 9.6%[6,8,9]

1 ml/L drinking water for 10 days or 1 ml/7 kg *q* 24h for 5 days PO

Carbaryl 5% powder[6,8,12]

Dust lightly once or twice weekly — May also be used to treat environment.

Fenbendazole[6,12]

20 mg/kg *q* 24h for 5 days PO

Ivermectin[6–10,12,15]

0.2–0.4 mg/kg *q* 7–14 days PO, SC — For treatment of *Psoroptes* and *Cheyletiella*. May require dosages up to 1.0 mg/kg for resistant *Cheyletiella*.

Lime sulfur dip 2–3%[6,7,10]

Saturate coat once a week for 4–6 weeks; protect rabbit's eyes.

Mebendazole[8]

50 mg/kg *q* 24h for 14 days PO

Metronidazole[6,9,12,15]

20 mg/kg *q* 12h for 5 days PO — May be useful for treating Clostridial enteritis.

Monensin[8]

0.002–0.004% in feed

Niclosamide[8]

100 mg/kg *q* 24h for 21 days PO or 100 mg/kg *q* 7 days for 21 days PO

continued

Piperazine[6,9]
200 mg/kg PO, repeat in 2–3
weeks; or 100 mg/kg PO *q*
24h for 2 days

Praziquantel[6,8,12,15]
5–10 mg/kg PO, SC, IM;
repeat in 10 days

Pyrantel pamoate[7]
5–10 mg/kg PO; repeat in 2–3
weeks

**Pyrethrin 0.05% shampoo,
0.03% spray**[6]

Shampoo or spray once a week for 4–6 weeks.

Sulfadimethoxine[6,8,9]
50 mg/kg PO once; then 25
mg/kg *q* 24h for 9 days PO

Sulfamerazine[12]
100 mg/kg PO

Sulfamethazine[11,12]
100 mg/kg PO or 1,000 mg/L
drinking water

Sulfaquinoxaline[6–8,11,12,15]
0.025–0.15% in drinking
water at 1,000 mg/L
drinking water

Thiabendazole[6,8,12]
50–100 mg/kg *q* 24h for
5 days PO

ANESTHETIC AND ANALGESIC AGENTS

DRUG DOSE AND ROUTE   COMMENTS

Acepromazine maleate[8,19]
0.5–1.0 mg/kg SC, IM

Aspirin[6,8,10,12]
100 mg/kg q 4–6h PO

Atropine sulfate

| | Serum atropinesterase occurs in approximately 30% of rabbits and will limit efficacy. |
0.1–3.0 mg/kg SC[8]   Preanesthetic dose.
10 mg/kg q 20 min SC[12]   For treatment of organophosphate toxicity.

Buprenorphine hydrochloride[8,10]
0.01–0.1 mg/kg q 8–12h SC, IM, IV

Butorphanol[8,10,12]
0.1–0.5 mg/kg q 4h SC, IM, IV

Carprofen
2 mg/kg q 12h SC, PO   Muscle necrosis occurs with IM injection.

Cosequin
1/2 capsule q 12h PO

Diazepam[8,12]
1–3 mg/kg IM

Fentanyl-droperidol[8,10,12,19]
0.13–0.22 mg/kg IM

Flunixin meglumine[6,10,19]
1–2 mg/kg q 12h SC, IM   Use for up to 3–5 days; contraindicated with renal compromise.

continued

Glycopyrrolate[8,19]

10 mcg/kg (0.01–0.02 mg/kg)
IM

Ibuprofen[8,12]

10–20 mg/kg *q* 4h or as
needed, PO

Ketamine hydrochloride[8]

10 mg/kg IV or 20–40 mg/kg   Causes local muscle irritation; results in variable
SC, IM   analgesia and muscle relaxation.

**Ketamine +
acepromazine**[10,12,19]

25–40 mg ketamine/kg +
0.25–1.0 mg
acepromazine/kg IM

Ketamine + diazepam[9,10,19]

20–30 mg ketamine/kg +
1–3 mg diazepam/kg IM or
10 mg ketamine/kg +
0.5 mg diazepam/kg IV

Ketamine + midazolam[8]

25 mg ketamine/kg + 1.0 mg
midazolam/kg IM or
intranasally

Ketamine + xylazine[10,12,19]

20–40 mg ketamine/kg + 3 mg
xylazine/kg IM or 10 mg
ketamine/kg + 3 mg
xylazine/kg IV

Ketamine + xylazine + acepromazine[8]
35 mg ketamine/kg + 3 mg xylazine/kg + 0.75 mg acepromazine/kg IM

May cause severe hypotension, bradycardia, and respiratory depression.

Ketamine + xylazine + butorphanol[8]
35 mg ketamine/kg + 5 mg xylazine/kg + 0.1 mg butorphanol/kg IM

Ketoprofen[12]
1.0 mg/kg q 8–12h IM

Midazolam[8]
1–2 mg/kg IM

Duration of action is approximately 15 minutes.

Morphine[12,19]
2–5 mg/kg q 2–4h SC, IM

Nalbuphine[12]
1–2 mg/kg q 4h SC, IM

Nalorphine[8,15]
1–5 mg/kg IM

For narcotic reversal.

Naloxone[6]
0.01–0.10 mg/kg IM, IV

For narcotic reversal.

Oxymorphone[19]
0.05–0.2 mg/kg q 8–12h SC, IM

Pentazocaine[12,19]
5–10 mg/kg q 2–4h SC, IM

continued

Pentobarbital sodium[8,19]

20–45 mg/kg IV, IP

Dilute in saline for administration. Not recommended for surgical anesthesia; provides limited analgesia. Recovery prolonged with glucose administration.

Propofol[8,20,21]

5–15 mg/kg IV for induction, then 0.8–1.3 mg/kg/min for maintenance anesthesia

Decreases cardiac output; may cause apnea and respiratory arrest.

Tiletamine-zolazepam[8,19]

3–15 mg/kg IM

May cause nephrotoxicity.

Xylazine hydrochloride[8,19]

1–3 mg/kg IM

May cause severe hypotension. Can be reversed with 0.2 mg yohimbine/kg IV.

Yohimbine[19]

0.2–1.0 mg/kg IM, IV

For reversal of xylazine.

MISCELLANEOUS AGENTS

DRUG DOSE AND ROUTE	COMMENTS

Calcium EDTA[6,12]

27.5 mg/kg q 6h SC

Dilute in saline; do not mix with Lactated Ringer's Solution.

Cholestyramine[8]

2 g/20 ml water q 24h PO or by gavage

Ion exchange for toxin absorption or inappropriate antibiotic administration.

Cimetidine[6,15]

5–10 mg/kg q 8–12h PO, SC, IM, IV

Dilute and administer slowly for IV use. With all routes of administration, decrease dose or frequency in renal compromise.

Cisapride[6,12]

0.5–1 mg/kg q 8h PO

Dexamethasone[8,12]
0.5–2.0 mg/kg q 12h PO, SC,   Use cautiously and taper rapidly; may lead to
IM, IV   signs of pasteurellosis or gastric ulceration.

Dexamethasone sodium phosphate
2–4 mg/kg IV   Used to stabilize cell membranes and decrease
                                 swelling in conditions of shock or central
                                 nervous system trauma.

Dextrose 50%[12]
2 ml/kg IV   Administer as a slow bolus for hypoglycemia.

Dipyrone[6,10,12]
6–12 mg/kg q 8–12h PO, IM

Doxapram[12]
2–5 mg/kg q 15 min SC, IV

Furosemide[6,12]
2–5 mg/kg q 12h or as
needed, PO, SC, IM, IV

Human chorionic gonadotropin[8]
20–25 IU IM

Meclizine[8]
2–12 mg/kg q 12–24h PO   Antiemetic; for use with vestibular signs.

Metoclopramide[6,8,10,12]
0.5–1.0 mg/kg q 8–12h PO,
SC

Oxytocin[6,12]
1–3 IU/kg as needed, SC, IM

Prednisone[6,12]
0.5–2.0 mg/kg PO, SC, IM

**Prednisone sodium
succinate**
25–30 mg/kg IV — Used to stabilize cell membranes and decrease swelling in conditions of shock or central nervous system trauma.

Tresaderm otic solution[6]
2–3 drops in affected ear q 12h

Verapamil[8,10,22]
2.5 mcg/kg/h IP or 0.2 mg/kg q 8h for 9 doses SC — Used to decrease the incidence of adhesion formation.

Viokase[6]
2–3 ml of yogurt mix q 12h PO — Mix 1 tsp viokase in 3 tbsp yogurt.

Vitamin K_1[6,12]
1–10 mg/kg as needed, PO, SC, IM — May need to continue treatment for 4–6 weeks in warfarin toxicity.

References

1. Plumb, D.C. Veterinary drug handbook. White Bear Lake, MN: PharmaVet Publishing; 1991.

2. Campbell, B.G., Bartholow, S., and Rosin, E. Bacterial killing by use of once daily gentamicin dosage in guinea pigs with *Escherichia coli* infection. Am J Vet Res 57:1627–1630; 1996.

3. Godber, L.M., Walker, R.D., Stein, G.E., Hauptman, J.G., and Derksen, F.J. Pharmacokinetics, nephrotoxicosis, and in vitro antibacterial activity associated with single versus multiple (three times) daily gentamicin treatments in horses. Am J Vet Res 56:613–618; 1995.

4. McClure, J.T., and Rosin, E. Comparison of amikacin dosing regimens in neutropenic guinea pigs with *Escherichia coli* infection. Am J Vet Res 59:750–755; 1998.

5. Okerman, L., DeVriese, L.A., Gevaert, D., Uyttebroek, D., and Haesebrouck, F. In vivo activity of orally administered antibiotics and chemotherapeutics against acute septicemic pasteurellosis in rabbits. Lab Animal 24:341–344; 1990.

6. Smith, D.A., and Burgmann, P.M. Formulary. In Hillyer, E.V., and Quesenberry, K.E., eds., Ferrets, rabbits, and rodents: Clinical medicine and surgery, pp. 392–403. Philadelphia: W.B. Saunders; 1997.

7. Quesenberry, K.E. Rabbits. In Birchard, S.J., and Scherding, R.D., eds., Saunders manual of small animal practice, pp. 1345–1362. Philadelphia: W.B. Saunders; 1994.

8. Harkness, J.E., and Wagner, J.E. The biology and medicine of rabbits and rodents, 4th ed. Philadelphia: Williams and Wilkins; 1995.

9. Hillyer, E.V. Pet rabbits. Vet Clin North Am/Small Anim Pract 24: 25–65; 1994.

10. Jenkins, J.R., and Brown, S.A. A practitioner's guide to rabbits and ferrets. Lakewood, CO: AAHA Press; 1993.

11. Burgmann, P., and Percy, D.H. Antimicrobial drug use in rodents and rabbits. In Prescott, J.F., and Baggot, J.D., eds., Antimicrobial therapy in veterinary medicine, 2nd ed., pp. 524–541. Ames: Iowa State University Press; 1993.

12. Johnson-Delaney, C.A. Exotic companion medicine handbook. Lake Worth, FL: Wingers Publishing; 1996.

13. Broome, R.L., Brooks, D.L., Babish J.G., Copeland, D.D., and Conzelman, G.H. Pharmacokinetic properties of enrofloxacin in rabbits. Am J Vet Res 53:1835–1841; 1991.

14. Cabanes, A., Arboix, M., Garcia-Anton, J.M., and Rieg, F. Pharmacokinetics of enrofloxacin after intravenous and intramuscular injection in rabbits. Am J Vet Res 53:2090–2093; 1992.

15. Carpenter, J.W., Mashima, T.Y., and Rupiper, D.J. Exotic animal formulary. Manhattan, KS: Greystone; 1996.

16. Nickolau, D.P., Freeman, C.D., Nightingale, C.H., and Quintiliani, R. Pharmacokinetics of minocycline and vancomycin in rabbits. Lab Anim Sci 43:222–225; 1993.

17.   Collins, B. Antimicrobial drug use in rabbits, rodents, and other small mammals. In Antimicrobial therapy in caged birds and exotic pets, pp. 3–10. Trenton, NJ:Veterinary Learning Systems; 1995.

18.   McElroy, D.E., Ravis, W.R., and Clark, C.H. Pharmacokinetics of oxytetracycline hydrochloride in rabbits. Am J Vet Res 48:1261–1263; 1987.

19.   Mason, D.E. Anesthesia, analgesia, and sedation for small mammals. In Hillyer, E.V., and Quesenberry, K.E., eds., Ferrets, rabbits, and rodents: Clinical medicine and surgery, pp. 378–391. Philadelphia: W.B. Saunders; 1997.

20.   Aeschbacher, G., and Webb, A.I. Propofol in rabbits. 1. Determination of an induction dose. Lab Anim Sci 43:324–327; 1993.

21.   Aeschbacher, G., and Webb, A.I. Propofol in rabbits. 2. Long-term anesthesia. Lab Anim Sci 43:328–335; 1993.

22.   Steinleitner, A., Lambert, H., Kazensky, C., Sanchez, I., and Sueldo, C. Reduction of primary postoperative adhesion formation under calcium channel blockade in the rabbit. J Surg Res 48:42–45; 1990.

Reptilian and Amphibian Drug Dosages

Thomas H. Boyer, DVM

General Guidelines

Drug use in reptiles and amphibians has traditionally been heavily empirical. Most studies on the use of antibiotics in reptiles present preliminary results derived from short antibiotic trials. Little is known about long-term drug accumulation, yet the slow metabolism of reptiles often dictates long-term drug usage. For instance, bacterial infections are typically treated for a minimum of 3 weeks. With so little known, it behooves the practitioner to observe some basic guidelines.

1. Use antibiotics only when there is a strong likelihood of bacterial infection; avoid antibiotic usage to placate clients.[1] Instead of relying on antibiotics to treat an unknown disease, utilize diagnostics to find out what the problem is.[1]

2. Start treatment as early as possible after having taken samples for bacterial culture and sensitivity.[1] The presence of multiple bacteria, with multiple antibiotic resistance, is the norm for infections in reptiles.[1] Anaerobic infections are quite common,[2] yet the most frequently used antibiotics in reptiles, fluoroquinolones and aminoglycosides, are relatively useless against anaerobes. Antibiotics recommended for use against anaerobes in reptiles include carbenicillin, ceftazidime,

and metronidazole.[3] Sensitivity testing allows one to select the right antibiotic well before a clinical response is apparent. Avoid frequent switching of antibiotics.

3. Select bactericidal antibiotics over bacteriostatic antibiotics[4] unless sensitivity testing dictates otherwise. It is preferable to use antibiotics, when possible, backed by some reptilian pharmacokinetic data.

4. Some reptiles have a renal portal system with valves that allow blood to be shunted through or around the kidneys. Therefore, drugs injected in the hind region of reptiles could circulate through the kidneys before reaching the systemic circulation or bypass the kidneys altogether. Theoretically, this mechanism could reduce the therapeutic levels of drugs that are excreted through the kidneys or increase the nephrotoxicity of certain drugs. A study by Holz and colleagues[5] supports the presence of a renal portal system in red-eared sliders. The investigators found that forelimb versus hindlimb injection had no significant effect on gentamicin, a drug excreted through glomerular filtration. In contrast, differences were found for carbenicillin, a drug excreted by glomerular filtration and tubular secretion. Turtles injected with carbenicillin in the rear limbs had significantly lower blood levels of carbenicillin for the first 12 hours after injection than those injected in the forelimbs. Even though the differences were statistically significant, the minimal inhibitory concentrations (MICs) from both sites were high enough to be effective for most organisms treated with carbenicillin, and thus the therapeutic effect was similar for both sites.[5] This study indicates that the renal portal system may have effects on drugs excreted

through tubular secretion, but the significance of those
effects are unknown. Until more is known, it is best to give
drugs that are excreted through the kidneys in the front half
of reptiles, thereby avoiding the necessity to consider the
nephrotoxic or tubular secretion potential.[6]

5. When calculating drug doses for chelonians, do not
adjust for shell weight because the shell is likely to be metabolically active.[7]

6. Because reptiles are ectothermic, the pharmacokinetics
of drugs used in reptiles are heavily influenced by ambient
temperature. Numerous studies[8–11] have shown that drug
clearance is slower at lower environmental temperatures
(because of lower metabolic rate), which can lead to drug
accumulation and potential toxicity. It is crucially important
that reptiles be acclimated and maintained within their preferred optimum temperature zone (POTZ) while they are
being treated with potentially nephrotoxic drugs.[11] In addition, one study found that the MICs for some bacterial
pathogens were lower at 37°C (98.6°F) than at 25°C
(77°F).[10] Therefore, increased temperature may not only
increase immune system activity but also enhance antibiotic
effectiveness. Thus, it is a good idea to select temperatures
within the POTZ that reasonably coincide with temperatures from pharmacokinetic studies.[12] The POTZ for many
species is from 24 to 30°C (75 to 85°F), but sick reptiles do
better between 27 and 32°C (80 and 90°F). In the veterinary
hospital it is best to dedicate a room for reptiles heated to
the desired temperature. Alternatives are incubators or heat-
ing pads kept at the desired temperature. Be aware that temperatures over 38°C (100°F) are rapidly lethal for many

reptiles and that debilitated reptiles are sometimes too weak to move from a heat source. Therefore, temperatures and animals must be monitored closely to avoid overheating, dehydration, or death. Unfortunately, temperature affects not only metabolic rate but also blood and tissue pH (pH drops with increasing temperature), which in turn affects antibiotic bioavailability and toxicity.[13] This may explain the increased gentamicin nephrotoxicity at higher temperatures that Hodge observed in water snakes,[9,13] or perhaps it is a reflection of increased susceptibility to toxicity of more metabolically active cells.

7.   Most drug use in reptiles and amphibians is extra-label. With the great diversity of species and ecologies, major differences in drug use and effect are likely to occur for different reptiles and amphibians. What applies to one species may not prove true in another species. Nonetheless, one is faced with the situation of frequently having to extrapolate known reptilian pharmacokinetics from one species to another. Use potentially toxic drugs with extreme caution and avoid long-term usage. Also bear in mind that aminoglycosides and enrofloxacin may accumulate in a stepwise fashion over time.[14]

Additional Guidelines for Specific Drugs

Aminoglycosides

Aminoglycosides function poorly in abscesses, in the presence of exudates, under conditions of low oxygen availability such as hypoxic tissue, and against anaerobes. Two aminoglycosides have been investigated in reptiles, gentamicin and amikacin. For both, there is little antibiotic resistance (less than 10% in one study).[15] Of the two, gentamicin is widely assumed to have a much narrower therapeutic index. Gentamicin-induced nephrotoxicity has been documented in snakes.[16,17] The likelihood of nephrotoxicity can be reduced by avoiding aminoglycoside usage in dehydrated patients, maintaining good hydration during treatment, and monitoring plasma uric acids before, during, and 2 weeks after the last treatment. Unfortunately, plasma uric acid levels are an insensitive indicator of renal disease, as two thirds of the functional renal mass must be lost before blood levels of uric acid become elevated.[14] Elevated plasma uric acid levels should be cause for concern.[18,19] Because some snakes and carnivorous lizards have elevated uric acid levels for several days postprandially, it might be advantageous to minimize feeding when clinical conditions permit this.[18] It is important to ensure adequate hydration by providing suitable access to water and to consider 15 to 25 ml/kg of fluids via gavage, subcutaneously, or epi- or intracoelomically.[19,20] Although additional fluids may not be required, they certainly would do no harm. In addition, pay attention to ambient temperatures and match those closely to the temperatures of known pharmacokinetic trials. As aminoglycosides appear to accumulate in a stepwise fashion over time, therapy for longer than 2 weeks is particularly worrisome.[21] Johnson et al.[14] recommended only a single dose of amikacin because of concern about nephrotoxicity. Transcutaneous absorption of aminoglycosides is possible in amphibians, but erratic serum levels and toxicity contraindicate this method of delivery.[22] Aminoglycosides should not be used in conjunction with loop diuretics such as furosemide, and combination with carbenicillin, ticarcillin, or piperacillin is problematic (see below). Given the safety of other broad-spectrum antibiotics, aminoglycosides are not typically the author's choice for reptiles.

Penicillins and Cephalosporins

These drugs generally have broad-spectrum bactericidal activity against a variety of aerobic and anaerobic pathogens; unfortunately, they tend to be expensive (except for ampicillin). One study found 85% of reptilian aerobic bacterial isolates to be resistant to ampicillin; only 35% were resistant to carbenicillin.[15] Ceftazidime appears to be a highly effective drug against *Pseudomonas*.[23] Penicillins and cephalosporins have a much safer therapeutic index than the aminoglycosides and may be synergistic in combination with aminoglycosides. However, combination therapy involves some inherent difficulties, such as the potential inactivation of gentamicin by carbenicillin. These drugs should not be mixed in a syringe and the dosages should be staggered. Jacobson[3,18] recommended starting ceftazidime or carbenicillin 24 or 48 hours (respectively) after aminoglycoside administration. Once reconstituted, many semisynthetic penicillins have a shelf life of 72 hours if refrigerated, but they can be aliquoted and frozen for longer usage. Note that carbenicillin causes pain on injection.[13]

Chloramphenicol

The bacteriostatic nature of this drug makes it less useful than bactericidal antibiotics in reptiles. It is, however, beneficial for treating several anaerobes and *Salmonella* and when the sensitivity pattern leaves no alternatives. Most *Pseudomonas* are resistant to it. Note that there is a wide variation among species in dosing intervals. In one study, one of nine water snakes (*Nerodia* spp.) developed greenish plasma after 9 days of chloramphenicol (CHPC) administration at 50 mg/kg SC *q* 72h and was anemic when the packed cell volume was checked on day 18 of the study.[24] Focal indurations may develop at the injection site of CHPC preparations suspended in propylene glycol and benzyl alcohol.[18]

Fluoroquinolones

These drugs have good gram-negative aerobic activity as well as effectiveness against *Mycoplasma* and *Mycobacteria*. *Pseudomonas* and *Citrobacter* spp. require higher minimal inhibitory concentrations, which can be achieved by decreasing the dosing interval or increasing the dosage. Fluoroquinolones have a wide spectrum of safety and little bacterial resistance at this time. Ciprofloxacin can be suspended in distilled water and given via gavage, which is practical for large snakes. Enrofloxacin is irritating when given SC or IM; therefore injection sites should be varied. Skin necrosis and permanent skin discoloration have developed in snakes. Oral enrofloxacin, either from crushed suspended tablets or in injectable form, produces good clinical results.

For Further Reading

For more in-depth discussions of therapeutics see Klingenberg,[20] Jacobson,[3] Mader,[19] and Carpenter et al.[25]

Drug Dosages for Reptiles and Amphibians

Antibiotics and Antifungal Agents
(Dosages based on limited pharmacokinetic studies)

DRUG DOSE AND ROUTE	SPECIES, TEMPERATURE, COMMENTS
Amikacin	
2.25 mg/kg q 72–96h IM	American alligator, *Alligator m. mississippiensis,* 22°C (72°F)[26]
5 mg/kg q 48h IM	Gopher tortoise, *Gopherus polyphemus,* 30°C (86°F)[11]
5 mg/kg IM initially, then 2.5 mg/kg q 72h IM	Gopher snake, *Pituophis melanoleucus* spp., 37°C (99°F)[10]
3.48 mg/kg IM once	Ball python, *Python regius,* 25°C (77°F) or 37°C (98.6°F)[14]
5 mg/kg IM (dosing interval unknown)	Bullfrog, *Rana catesbeiana.* Temperature not given. Serum drug levels above the MIC for most bacterial pathogens for 38 hours.[27]
Ampicillin	
50 mg/kg q 12h IM	Hermann's tortoise, *Testudo hermanni,* 27°C (81°F)[28]
Carbenicillin	
400 mg/kg q 24h IM	Mangrove snake, *Boiga dendrophilia,* King snake, *Lampropeltis g. getulus,* Reticulated python, *Python reticulatus,* Rat snakes, *Elaphe* spp., 30°C (86°F)[29]
400 mg/kg q 48h IM	Mediterranean tortoises, *Testudo graeca* and *T. hermanni,* 30°C (86°F)[30]

IM = intramuscularly
IV = intravenously
PO = per os; orally
SC = subcutaneously

Cefoperazone

100 mg/kg *q* 96h IM — False water cobra, *Hydrodynastes gigas,* 24°C (75°F)[31]

125 mg/kg *q* 24h IM — Black and white tegu, *Tupinambis teguixin,* 24°C (75°F)[32]

Ceftazidime

20 mg/kg *q* 72h IM — Mangrove snake, *Boiga dendrophilia,* Boids (pythons and boas), Rat snake, *Elaphe obsoleta* spp., 30°C (86°F)[23]

20 mg/kg *q* 72h IM, IV — Loggerhead sea turtles, *Caretta caretta,* 24°C (75°F)[33]

Chloramphenicol

40 mg/kg *q* 24h SC — Gopher snake, *Pituophis melanoleucus* spp., 29°C (84°F)[8]

50 mg/kg *q* 12h SC — Indigo snake, *Drymarchon* spp., Rat snake, *Elaphe* spp., King snakes, *Lampropeltis* spp., 24–28°C (75–82°F)[24]

50 mg/kg *q* 24h SC — Boa, *Boa constrictor,* Burmese python, *Python molorus bivittatus,* Copperhead and cottonmouth, *Agkistrodon* spp., Hog-nose snake, *Heterodon* spp., 24–28°C (75–82°F)[24]

50 mg/kg *q* 48h SC — Rattlesnakes, *Crotalus* spp., 24–28°C (75–82°F)[24]

50 mg/kg *q* 72h SC — Water snakes, *Nerodia* spp., 24–28°C (75–82°F)[24]

Ciprofloxacin

2.5 mg/kg *q* 48–72h PO — Reticulated python, *Python reticulatus,* 27°C (81°F)[34]

Clarithromycin

15 mg/kg *q* 48–72h PO — Desert tortoise, *Gopherus agassizii,* 30.0–33.3°C (86–92°F). New antimycoplasma drug.[35]

continued

91

Doxycycline

50 mg/kg IM (rear leg), then
25 mg/kg *q* 72h IM

Hermann's tortoise, *Testudo hermanni,* 27°C
(81°F)[28]

Enrofloxacin

6.6 mg/kg *q* 24h IM or
11 mg/kg *q* 48h IM

Reticulated pythons, *Python reticulatus,* 27°C
(81°F)[36]

10 mg/kg *q* 48h IM for
Pseudomonas

Burmese pythons, *Python molurus bivittatus,*
30°C (86°F)[37]

10 mg/kg IM initially, then
5 mg/kg *q* 48h IM for other
bacteria

Burmese pythons, *Python molurus bivittatus,*
30°C (86°F)[37]

5 mg/kg *q* 24–48h IM

Gopher tortoises, *Gopherus polyphemus,*
29–31°C (84–88°F)[38]

5 mg/kg *q* 12–24h IM

Star tortoises, *Geochelone elegans,* 26–30°C
(79–86°F)[39]

10 mg/kg *q* 24h IM

Hermann's tortoise, *Testudo hermanni,* 27°C
(81°F)[28]

5 mg/kg *q* 32h PO
5 mg/kg *q* 16h IM

Green iguana, *Iguana iguana.* Temperature not
given.[40]

10 mg/kg IM, PO (dosing
interval unknown)

Savanna monitor,*Varanus exanthematicus,*
26–28°C (78.8–82.4°F). Plasma drug levels
above the MIC for most bacterial pathogens for
36 hours (last sample time in study). Authors
suggest dosing every 5 days.[41]

5 mg/kg *q* 36h IV

American alligator,*Alligator m. mississippiensis,*
27°C (81°F)[42]

5 mg/kg IM (dosing interval
unknown)

Bullfrog, *Rana catesbeiana,* temperature not
given. Serum drug levels above the MIC for
most bacterial pathogens at 96 hours (last
sample time in study).[27]

Gentamicin

2.5 mg/kg *q* 72h IM
Gopher snake, *Pituophis melanoleucus* spp., 24°C (75°F)[8]

2.5 mg/kg IM initially, then 1.5 mg/kg *q* 96h IM
Blood python, *Python curtus,* 28–30°C (82–86°F)[43]

1.75 mg/kg *q* 72–96h IM
American alligator, *Alligator m. mississippiensis,* 22°C (72°F)[26]

6 mg/kg *q* 96–120h IM
Red-eared slider, *Chrysemys scripta elegans,* 23–25°C (73–77°F)[44]

3 mg/kg *q* 24h IM
Leopard frog, *Rana pipiens,* 22°C (72°F)[45]

2.5 mg/kg *q* 72h IM
Mud puppy, waterdog, *Necturus* spp., 2–3°C (36–37°F)[46]

Itraconazole

23.5 mg/kg *q* 24h PO for three treatments
Spiny lizards, *Sceloporus* spp., ambient temperature. Dosage maintains blood levels for another 5 days.[47]

Ketoconazole

15 mg/kg *q* 24h PO
Gopher tortoises, *Gopherus polyphemus,* 27°C (81°F)[48]

Metronidazole

20 mg/kg *q* 48h PO
Yellow rat snakes, *Elaphe obsoleta quadrivitatta.* Temperature not given.[49]

20 mg/kg *q* 24–48h PO
Green iguanas, *Iguana iguana,* 31–34°C (88–93°F)[50]

For anaerobic bacteria or protozoan overgrowth. Can give as whole tablets or crushed and suspended in water.[51] Discontinue if central nervous symptoms develop. For small patients, injectable metronidazole (Metronidazole Redi-infusion, 5 mg/ml, Elkin-Sinn Inc.) works well.[52]

continued

Oxytetracycline

50 mg/kg IM (dosing interval unknown)	Bullfrog, *Rana catesbeiana.* Temperature not given. Serum drug levels above the MIC for most bacterial pathogens for 96 hours (last sample time in study).[27]
10 mg/kg IV (dosing interval unknown)	American alligator, *Alligator m. mississippiensis,* 27°C (80.6°F)[42]

Piperacillin

80–100 mg/kg *q* 48h IM	Blood python, *Python curtus,* 28–30°C (82–86°F)[53]

ENDOPARASITIC AGENTS
(Empirically derived drug dosages)

DRUG DOSE AND ROUTE	COMMENTS
Fenbendazole	
25–100 mg/kg *q* 14d PO for four treatments	Drug of choice for nematodes.[54]
Ivermectin	
0.2 mg/kg *q* 14d PO, SC, for four treatments	Can cause neurologic symptoms in some species. Not recommended for skinks. **Do not use in chelonians.**[18,54]
2.0 mg/kg cutaneously (anterior dorsal coelom)	Treatment for nematodes in frogs.[55]
Metronidazole	
100 mg/kg PO once	For appetite stimulation.[4]
Oxfendazole	
65 mg/kg once via stomach tube	Efficacious wormer for tortoises.[56–58]
Praziquantel	
3–8 mg/kg PO, IM; repeat in 14 days	Drug of choice for trematodes.[18,59]

ECTOPARASITIC AGENTS
(Empirically derived drug dosages)

DRUG DOSE AND ROUTE	COMMENTS

Ivermectin

5 mg tap-water solution	Spray for mites. Do not use on chelonians. Mix new monthly.[60]

Permectrin II

0.007 to 0.002% spray *q* 14d for three treatments	Treatment for mites. Dilute from 10% stock solution (Permectrin II, Bio-Centric Division, Boehringer Ingelheim Animal Health Inc.) to 0.007% (5 ml in 710 ml tap water) to 0.002% (15 ml in 710 ml tap water) and use as spray. Make fresh for each treatment.[61]

METABOLIC BONE DISEASE TREATMENT
(Empirically derived drug dosages)

DRUG DOSE AND ROUTE	COMMENTS

Calcitonin

50 IU/kg/wk IM for two treatments	Part of treatment for metabolic bone disease (MBD). **Do not give if hypocalcemic** (plasma calcium < 8.5 mg/dl) or delay giving until 3 days of Neo-calglucon treatment.[62,63]

10% Calcium gluconate

100 mg/kg (100 mg/ml) *q* 6h intracoelomically	For control of hypocalcemic muscle tremors, seizures, or flaccid paresis in lizards. As soon as patient is stable, switch to oral Neo-calglucon.

Neo-calglucon
(Calcium glubionate)

1 ml/kg *q* 12h PO for 1–3 months	Part of treatment for MBD.[62,64]

continued

Vitamin D

1000 IU/kg IM for two treatments

Part of treatment for MBD.[60,64] Only indicated if history suggests vitamin D deficiency.

MISCELLANEOUS AGENTS
(Empirically derived drug dosages)

DRUG DOSE AND ROUTE	COMMENTS

Arginine vasotocin

0.01–1.0 mcg/kg IV or intracoelomically

More efficacious than oxytocin in stimulating oviposition. Short shelf life unless frozen. Expensive. Experimental drug license and number required (Sigma Chemicals).[65]

Oxytocin

2–10 IU/kg q 4–6h IM for one to three treatments

For egg retention. Works well in chelonians. Provide warm, quiet, darkened environment with appropriate nesting substrate. Oviductal rupture has been reported with multiple doses.[66]

Trimethoprim-sulfadiazine

30 mg/kg q 24h IM for two treatments, then q 48h IM

Good activity against gram-positive and gram-negative aerobes, especially in enteric infections. Not clear if bactericidal or bacteriostatic in reptiles.[18]

Vitamin A

2000 IU/kg q 7–14d SC, IM, for two to four treatments

For treatment of hypovitaminosis A if clinical signs and dietary history support diagnosis. Overdosage will cause epidermal sloughing; therefore, dose carefully.[4,52]

Vitamin B complex

25 mg/kg q 24h PO for three to seven treatments

For treatment of thiamine deficiency and appetite stimulation, dosed on thiamine content.[4]

ANESTHETIC AGENTS FOR REPTILES

DRUG DOSE AND ROUTE   COMMENTS

Isoflurane

Anesthesia of choice for surgery. Intubation and intermittent positive pressure ventilation advisable. Mask induction possible, or one can preanesthetize with low dose of ketamine, Telazol, propofol, or a medetomidine-ketamine combination. Use 1–3% for maintenance, 3–5% for induction. If intubation desired, premedicate with atropine sulfate (0.04 mg/kg SC or IM) or glycopyrrolate (0.01 mg/kg SC or IM), 30 minutes prior to intubation. Non-rebreathing circuit advisable for reptiles < 10 kg with a minimum oxygen flow rate of 300 to 500 ml/kg/min.; monitor EKG, pulse oximetry, or doppler blood flow. Spontaneous respiration can be delayed post-anesthesia; ventilate with room air until patient is breathing regularly.

For more extensive review of reptilian anesthesia, the reader is referred to Bennett,[67,68] Frye,[69] Lawton,[70] Schumacher,[71] and Boyer.[72,73]

Ketamine hydrochloride

Painful at injection site; some reptiles may have an immediate or delayed violent reaction from injection. Should not be used in animals with renal impairment. Larger reptiles are thought to require smaller mg/kg doses compared to smaller reptiles; this was not the case with red-eared sliders, however.[74] Use isoflurane for surgical anesthesia. Analgesia with ketamine hydrochloride is questionable. Local anesthetic should be used in conjunction with ketamine.[75–77]

30–50 mg/kg IM	Lizards, for light sedation; then go to isoflurane for anesthesia
20–60 mg/kg IM	Snakes, light sedation
60–80 mg/kg IM	Snakes, light anesthesia
50–70 mg/kg IM	Turtles, sedation (lower end of dose recommended for aquatic turtles)
70–100 mg/kg IM	Turtles, light anesthesia

continued

**Lidocaine hydrochloride,
Mepivicaine hydrochloride**

1–2% solution SC, IM — Infiltrate to effect. Analgesia within 3–5 minutes; duration of analgesia about 90 minutes.[78] Excellent for minor procedures.

**Medetomidine-ketamine
combination**

75 mcg/kg medetomidine IM +
7.5 mg/kg ketamine IM — Gopher tortoises, *Gopherus polyphemus.* Dosage provides enough anethesia to allow intubation at 14 to 33 minutes (mean = 23 minutes). Deep pain sensation is still present. Can reverse with atipamezole IM at 5 times the medetomidine dosage 60 minutes after medetomidine-ketamine combination. Tortoises almost completely recovered within 30 to 180 minutes (mean = 93 minutes).[79]

100 mcg/kg medetomidine
mixed with 5.0 mg/kg
ketamine IV in dorsal
coccygeal vein — Leopard and yellow foot tortoises *(Geochelone pardalis* and *G. denticulata).* Reversed with 400 mcg/kg atipamezone IV in the jugular vein 25 to 90 minutes after medetomidine-ketamine combination.[80]

25–80 mcg/kg medetomidine
mixed with 3.0–8.0 mg/kg
ketamine IV in dorsal
coccygeal vein — Aldabra tortoises, *Aldabrachelys (Geochelone) gigantea.* Reversed with 100–380 mcg/kg atipamezone IV in the jugular vein 25 to 90 minutes after medetomidine-ketamine combination.[80]

Induction time (time from drug injection until the head can be pulled out and mouth opened) for performing minor procedures ranged from 4 to 16 minutes (median = 10 minutes) for leopard and yellow foot tortoises and from 15 to 45 minutes (median = 45 minutes) for Aldabra tortoises. Recovery times (time from injection of atipamezole until tortoises were able to withdraw head into shell) ranged from 2 to 20 minutes (median = 5 minutes) for leopard and yellow foot tortoises and from 5 to 15 minutes (median = 5 minutes) for Aldabra tortoises. Two leopard tortoises vomited after atipamezole injection. Several tortoises exhibited transient bilateral hindlimb paralysis for several hours that may have been due to epidural administration.[80]

Propofol
Excellent short-acting anesthetic that is given to effect intravenously. The intravenous route of administration can be difficult. Propofol is a white opaque liquid that easily passes through small-gauge needles. It is not painful with injection and perivascular injection does not cause problems. Induction is rapid (within 1 to 5 minutes) and smooth recovery is complete within 25 to 40 minutes. Surgical anesthesia lasts 10 to 30 minutes, making this an excellent anesthetic for short procedures or induction. Twenty-milliliter ampules may be aliquoted under sterile conditions and frozen for future use. It is recommended that iguanas receiving propofol be intubated and ventilated with oxygen to avoid hypoxemia and hypercapnia. All patients should be intubated and ventilated if apnea develops. For more information see Lawton,[70] Divers,[81] Bennett et al.,[82] and Anderson et al.[83]

5–6 mg/kg IV or intracardiac	Snakes. Use higher dose in obese or agitated snakes.[83]
5–10 mg/kg IV or intraosseously	Lizards[70,82]
14 mg/kg IV	Chelonians[70]

Tiletamine hydrochloride–Zolazepam hydrochloride
Can be refrigerated for reuse up to a month after reconstitution. Severe respiratory depression possible; if apnea occurs, ventilate until animal is spontaneously breathing.[36,60,71,77]

3–15 mg/kg IM[84]	Crocodilians
5–10 mg/kg IM	Lizards, snakes
10–20 mg/kg IM	Turtles
5 mg/kg IM	Aquatic turtles

continued

ANALGESIC AGENTS FOR REPTILES

DRUG DOSE AND ROUTE	COMMENTS
Butorphanol	
0.4–1 mg/kg q 4–6h IM	Will cause sedation. Best to use preoperatively and for 2 to 3 days postoperatively. If given preoperatively will reduce amount of anesthetic required to maintain surgical anesthesia.[71,85]
Carprofen	
4 mg/kg IM initially; then 2–4 mg/kg q 48–72h IM	Observe same precautions as for use in mammals.[86]
Flunixin meglumine	
1–2 mg/kg IM once	Gastrointestinal ulceration is a concern with repeated usage.[68,85]

References

1. Lawrence, K. The use of antibiotics in reptiles: A review. J Small Anim Pract 24:741–752; 1983.

2. Stewart, J.S. Anaerobic bacterial infections in reptiles. J Zoo Wildl Med 21:180–184; 1990.

3. Jacobson, E.R. Use of antimicrobial therapy in reptiles. In Antimicrobial therapy in caged birds and exotics: An international symposium, pp. 28–37. Trenton, NJ: Veterinary Learning Systems; 1995.

4. Frye, F.L. Biomedical and surgical aspects of captive reptile husbandry. Malabar, FL: Krieger Publishing Company; 1991.

5.   Holz, P., Barker, I.K., Conlon, P.D., Crawshaw, G.J., and
     Burger, J. The reptilian renal portal system and its effects on
     drug kinetics. In Willette Frahm, ed., Proceedings of the
     American Association of Zoo Veterinarians, pp. 95–96. Pitts-
     burgh, PA: Association of Reptilian and Amphibian Veteri-
     narians; 1994.

6.   Mader, D.R. Personal communications; 1994 and 1996. Long
     Beach Animal Hospital, Long Beach, CA.

7.   Lawrence, K. Drug dosages for chelonians. Vet Rec 114:
     150–151; 1984.

8.   Bush, M., Smeller, J.M., Charache, P., and Soloron, H.M.
     Preliminary study of antibiotics in snakes. In Proceedings of
     the American Association of Zoo Veterinarians, pp. 50–54.
     St. Louis, MO: American Association of Zoo Veterinarians;
     1976.

9.   Hodge, M.K. The effect of acclimation temperature on gen-
     tamicin nephrotoxicity in the Florida banded water snake
     (*Natrix fasciata*). In American Association of Zoo Veterinari-
     ans Annual Proceedings, Vol. 78, pp. 226–237. Knoxville,
     TN: American Association of Zoo Veterinarians; 1978.

10. Mader, D.R., Conzelman, G.M., and Baggot, J.D. Effects of
     ambient temperature on the half-life and dosage regimen of
     amikacin in the gopher snake. J Am Vet Med Assoc
     187:1134–1136; 1985.

11. Caligiuri, R., Kollias, G.V., Jacobson, E., McNab, B., Clark,
     C.H., and Wilson, R.C. The effects of ambient temperature on
     amikacin pharmacokinetics in gopher tortoises. J Vet Pharma-
     col Ther 13:287–291; 1990.

12.   Jacobson, E.R. Use of antimicrobials in reptiles. Proceedings Arizona, California, Nevada Veterinary Conference; 1994.

13.   Lawrence, K. The use of drugs in reptiles. In Grunsell, G., Hill, F.W.G., and Raw, M., eds., Veterinary manual, 26th ed., pp. 366–371. Bristol, U.K.: John Wright & Sons; 1986.

14.   Johnson, J.H., Jensen, J.M., Brumbaugh, G.W., and Boothe, D.W. Amikacin pharmacokinetics and the effects of ambient temperature on the dosage regimen in ball pythons (*Python regius*). J Zoo Wildl Med 28:80–88; 1997.

15.   Beehler, B.A., and Sauro, A.M. Aerobic bacterial isolates and antibiotic sensitivities in a captive reptile population. In Proceedings of the Association of Zoo Veterinarians, pp. 198–200; 1983.

16.   Jacobson, E.R. Gentamicin-related visceral gout in two boid snakes. VetMed/Small Animal Clinic, March:361–363; 1976.

17.   Montali, R.J., Bush, M., and Smeller, J.M. The pathology of nephrotoxicity of gentamicin in snakes. Vet Pathol 16:108–115; 1979.

18.   Jacobson, E.R. Use of chemotherapeutics in reptile medicine. In Jacobson, E., and Kollias, G., Jr., eds. Exotic animals, pp. 35–48. New York: Churchill Livingstone; 1988.

19.   Mader, D.R. Antibiotic therapy in reptile medicine. In Frye, F.L., ed., Biomedical and surgical aspects of captive reptile husbandry, 2nd ed., Vol. 2, pp. 620–633. Malabar, FL: Krieger Publishing Company; 1991.

20.   Klingenberg, R.J. Therapeutics. In Mader, D.R., ed., Reptile medicine and surgery, pp. 299–321. Philadelphia: W.B. Saunders; 1996.

21. Bush, M., Smeller, J.M., Charach, P., and Arthur, R. Biological half-life of gentamicin in gopher snakes. Am J Vet Res 39:171–173; 1978.

22. Teare, J.A., and Bush, M. Toxicity and efficacy of ivermectin in chelonians. J Am Vet Med Assoc 183:1195–1197; 1983.

23. Lawrence, K., Muggleton, P.W., and Needham, J.R. Preliminary study on the use of ceftazidime, a broad spectrum cephalosporin antibiotic, in snakes. Res Vet Sci 36:16–20; 1984.

24. Clark, C.H., Rogers, E.D., and Milton, J.L. Plasma concentrations of chloramphenicol in snakes. Am J Vet Res 46:2654–2657; 1985.

25. Carpenter, J.W., Mashima, T.Y., and Rupiper, D.J. Amphibians and reptiles. In Exotic animal formulary, pp. 31–89. Manhattan, KS: Greystone; 1996.

26. Jacobson, E.R., Brown, M.P., Chung, M., Vliet, K., and Swift, R. Serum concentration and disposition kinetics of gentamicin and amikacin in juvenile American alligators. J Zoo Anim Med 19:188–194; 1988.

27. Letcher, J., and Papich, M. Pharmacokinetics of intramuscular administration of three antibiotics in bullfrogs, *Rana catesbeiana*. In Junge, R.E., ed., Proceedings of the American Association of Zoo Veterinarians, pp. 79–93. Pittsburgh, PA; 1994.

28. Sporle, H., Gobel, T., and Schildger, B. Blood levels of some antiinfectives in the spur-tailed tortoise (*Testudo hermanni*). Proceedings of the 4th International Colloquium on Pathology and Medicine of Repiles and Amphibians, Bad Nauheim, Germany; 1991. Abstract.

29. Lawrence, K., Needham, J.R., Palmer, G.H., and Lewis, J.C. A preliminary study on the use of carbenicillin in snakes. J Vet Pharmacol Ther 7:119–124; 1984.

30. Lawrence, K., Palmer, G.H., and Needham, J.R. Use of carbenicillin in two species of tortoise (*Testudo graeca* and *T. hermanni*). Res Vet Sci 40:413–415; 1986.

31. Speroni, J.A., Soraci, A., Giambeluca, L., and Errecalde, J.O. Farmacocinetica de cefoperazona tras su administracion intramuscular a *Hydrodynastes gigas* (Ophidia, Colubridae). AHA Communications Meeting, Buenos Aires, Argentina, 1989.

32. Speroni, J.A., Soraci, A., Giambeluca, L., and Errecalde, J.O. Farmacocinetica de cefoperazona tras su administracion intramuscular a *Tupinambis teguixin* (Sauria, Teidae). AHA Communications Meeting, Buenos Aires, Argentina, 1989.

33. Stamper, M.A., Papich, M.G., Lewbart, G.A., May, S.B., Plummer, D.D., and Stoskopf, M.K. Pharmacokinetics of ceftazidime in loggerhead sea turtles (*Caretta caretta*) after single intravenous and intramuscular injections. J Zoo Wildl Med 30:32–35; 1999.

34. Klingenberg, R.J., and Backner, B. The use of ciprofloxacin, a new antibiotic in snakes. In Uricheck, M.J., ed., Proceedings of the 15th International Herpetological Symposium on Captive Propagation Husbandry, pp. 127–140. Seattle, WA: International Herpetological Symposium; 1991.

35. Wimsatt, J., Johnson, J., Mangone, B.A., Tothill, A., Childs, J.M., and Peloquin, C.A. Clarithromycin pharmacokinetics in the desert tortoise (*Gopherus agassizii*). J Zoo Wildl Med 30:36–43; 1999.

36. Klingenberg, R.J. Personal communication; 1994. Sheep
     Draw Veterinary Hospital, Greeley, CO.

37. Young, L.E., Schumacher, J., Jacobson, E.R., and Papich, M.
     Disposition of enrofloxacin and its metabolite ciprofloxacin
     after intramuscular injection in juvenile Burmese pythons
     (*Python molorus bivittatus*). J Zoo Wildl Med 28:71; 1997.

38. Prezant, R.M., Isaza, R., and Jacobson, E.R. Plasma concen-
     trations and disposition kinetics of enrofloxacin in gopher tor-
     toises (*Gopherus polyphemus*). J Zoo Wildl Med 25:82–87;
     1994.

39. Raphael, B.L., Papich, M., and Cook, R.A. Pharmocokinetics
     of enrofloxacin after a single intramuscular injection in
     Indian star tortoises (*Geochelone elegans*). J Zoo Wildl Med
     25:88–94; 1994.

40. Maxwell, L.K., and Jacobson, E.R. Preliminary single-dose
     pharmacokinetics of enrofloxacin after oral and intramuscular
     administration in green iguanas (*Iguana iguana*). In Baer,
     C.K., ed., Proceedings of the American Association of Zoo
     Veterinarians, p. 25. Houston, TX: American Association of
     Zoo Veterinarians; 1997.

41. Hungerford, M.S., Spelman, L., and Papich, M. Pharmacoki-
     netics of enrofloxacin after oral and intramuscular adminis-
     tration in Savana monitors, *Varanus exanthematicus*. In Baer,
     C.K., ed., Proceedings of the American Association of Zoo
     Veterinarians, pp. 89–92. Houston, TX; American Associa-
     tion of Zoo Veterinarians; 1997.

42. Helmick, K.E., Papich, M.G., Vliet, K.A., Bennett, R.A., Brown, M.R., and Jacobson, E.R. Preliminary kinetics of single-dose intravenously administered enrofloxacin and oxytetracycline in the American alligator (*Alligator mississipiensis*). In Baer, C.K., ed., Proceedings of the American Association of Zoo Veterinarians, pp. 27–28. Houston, TX: American Association of Zoo Veterinarians; 1997.

43. Hilf, M., Swanson, D., Wagner, R., and Yu, V.L. A new dosing schedule for gentamicin in blood pythons (*Python curtus*): A pharmacokinetic study. Res Vet Sci 50:127–130; 1991.

44. Raphael, B., Clark, C.H., and Hudson, R. Plasma concentration of gentamicin in turtles. J Zoo Anim Med 16:136–139; 1985.

45. Teare, J.A., Wallace, R.S., and Bush, M. Pharmacology of gentamicin in the leopard frog (*Rana pipiens*). In Proceedings of the American Association of Zoo Veterinarians, pp. 128–131; 1991.

46. Stoskopf, M.K., Arnold, J., and Mason, M. Aminoglycoside antibiotic levels in the aquatic salamander *Necturus necturus*. J Zoo Anim Med 18:81–85; 1987.

47. Gamble, K.C., Alvarado, T.P., and Bennett, C.L. Plasma itraconazole pharmacokinetics in spiny lizards (*Scoloporus* spp.) from once daily dosing. In Baer, C.K., ed., Proceedings of the American Association of Zoo Veterinarians, pp. 245–246. Puerto Vallarta, Mexico: American Association of Zoo Veterinarians; 1996.

48. Page, D.C., Mautino, M., Derendorf, H., and Mechlinski, W.
     Multiple-dose pharmacokinetics of ketoconazole adminis-
     tered orally to gopher tortoises (*Gopherus polyphemus*).
     J Zoo Wildl Med 22:191–198; 1991.

49. Kolmstetter, C.K., Frazier, D., Cox, S., and Ramsay, E.C.
     Metronidazole pharmacokinetics in yellow rat snakes (*Elaphe
     obsoleta quadrivitatta*). In Proceedings of the American
     Association of Zoo Veterinarians, p. 26. Houston, TX: Amer-
     ican Association of Zoo Veterinarians; 1997.

50. Kolmstetter, C.K., Frazier, D., Cox, S., and Ramsay, E.C.
     Pharmacokinetics of metronidazole in the green iguana
     (*Iguana iguana*). Bull Assoc Rept Amphib Vet 9(3):4–7;
     1998.

51. Holt, P.E. Drugs and dosages. In Cooper, J.E., and Jackson,
     O.F., eds., Diseases of the reptilia, Vol. 2, pp. 551–584.
     London: Academic Press; 1981.

52. Boyer, T.H. Practitioner's guide to reptilian husbandry and
     care. Lakewood, CO: American Animal Hospital Associa-
     tion; 1993.

53. Hilf, M., Swanson, D., Wagner, R., and Yu, V.L. Pharmacoki-
     netics of piperacillin in blood pythons (*Python curtus*) and in
     vitro evaluation of efficacy against aerobic gram-negative
     bacteria. J Zoo Wildl Med 22:199–203; 1991.

54. Klingenberg, R.J. A comparison of fenbendazole and iver-
     mectin for the treatment of nematode parasites in ball
     pythons, *Python regius*. Bull Assoc Rept Amphib Vet
     2(2):5–6; 1992.

55. Letcher, J., and Glade, M. Efficacy of ivermectin as an anthelmintic in leopard frogs. J Am Vet Med Assoc 200:537–538; 1992.

56. McArthur, S. Veterinary management of tortoises and turtles. Oxford, England: Blackwell Science; 1996.

57. Pokras, M.A., Sedgwick, C.J., and Kaufman, G.E. Therapeutics. In Beynon, P.H., Lawton, M.P.C., and Cooper, J.E., eds., Manual of reptiles, p. 203. Cheltenham, England: British Small Animal Vet. Assoc.; 1992.

58. Divers, S.J. Captive husbandry of Mediterranean tortoises (*Testudo graeco* and *Testudo hermanni*). In Willette Frahm, M., ed., Proceedings of the Association of Reptilian and Amphibian Veterinarians, pp. 31–35. Tampa, FL; 1996.

59. Lawerence, K. Praziquantel as a taeniacide in snakes. Vet Rec 113:200; 1983.

60. Abrahams, R. Ivermectin as a spray for treatment of snake mites. Bull Assoc Rept Amphib Vet 2(1):8; 1992.

61. Boyer, D. Snake mite (*Ophionyssus natricus*) eradication utilizing permectrin spray. Bull Assoc Rept Amphib Vet 4(2):3;1994.

62. Boyer, T.H. Metabolic bone disease: Hypovitaminosis A. In Mader, D.R., ed., Reptile medicine and surgery, pp. 382–392. Philadelphia: W.B. Saunders; 1995.

63. Mader, D.R. Use of calcitonin in green iguanas, *Iguana iguana*, with metabolic bone disease. Bull Assoc Rept Amphib Vet 3(1):5; 1993.

64. Mader, D.R. Personal communication; 1994. Long Beach Animal Hospital, Long Beach, CA.

65.   Lloyd, M. Vasotocin—the reptilian alternative to oxytocin?
      Bull Assoc Rept Amphib Vet 2(1):5; 1992.

66.   Barten, S.L. Oviductal rupture in a Burmese python (*Python
      molorus bivittatus*) treated with oxytocin for egg retention.
      J Zoo Anim Med 16:141–143; 1985.

67.   Bennet, R.A. A review of anesthesia and chemical restraint in
      reptiles. J Zoo Wildl Med 22:282–303; 1991.

68.   Bennett, R.A. Anesthesia. In Mader, D.R., ed., Reptile medicine
      and surgery, pp. 241–247. Philadelphia: W.B. Saunders; 1996.

69.   Frye, F.L. Biomedical and surgical aspects of captive reptile
      husbandry, 2nd ed., Vols. 1 and 2. Malabar, FL: Krieger Pub-
      lishing Company; 1991.

70.   Lawton, M.P.C. Anesthesia. In Beynon, P.H., Lawton,
      M.P.C., and Cooper, J.E., eds., Manual of reptiles,
      pp. 170–183. Gloucestershire: England: British Small Animal
      Vet. Assoc.; 1992.

71.   Schumacher, J. Reptiles and amphibians. In Thurman, J.C.,
      Tranquilli, W.J., and Benson, G.J., eds., Lumb and Jones' vet-
      erinary anesthesia, 3rd ed., pp. 670–685. Baltimore, MD:
      Williams & Wilkins; 1996.

72.   Boyer, T.H. A practitioner's guide to reptilian husbandry and
      care. Lakewood, CO: American Animal Hospital Associa-
      tion; 1993.

73.   Boyer, T.H. Anethesia of reptiles. In Boyer, T.H., ed., Essen-
      tials of reptiles: A guide for practitioners, pp. 155–162. Lake-
      wood, CO: AAHA Press.

74. Holz, P., and Holz, R.M. Evaluation of ketamine, ketamine/ xylazine and ketamine/midazolam anesthesia in red-eared sliders, *Trachemys scripta elegans*. J Zoo Wildl Med 25:531–537; 1994.

75. Boyer, T.H. Clinical anesthesia of reptiles. Bull Assoc Rept Amphib Vet 2(2):10–13; 1992.

76. Millichamp, N. Surgical techniques in reptiles. In Jacobson, E., and Kollias, G., Jr., eds. Exotic animals, pp. 49–59. New York: Churchill Livingstone; 1988.

77. Johnson, J. Anesthesia, analgesia, and euthanasia of reptiles and amphibians. In Proceedings of the American Association of Zoo Veterinarians, pp. 132–138; 1991.

78. Mader, D.R. Understanding local analgesics: Practical use in the green iguana, *Iguana iguana*. In Willette Frahm, M., ed., Proceedings of the Association of Reptilian and Amphibian Veterinarians, pp. 7–10. Kansas City, MO; 1998.

79. Norton, T.M., Spratt, J., Behler, J., and Hernandez, K. Medetomidine and ketamine anesthesia with atipamezole reversal in private free-ranging gopher tortoises, *Gopherus polyphemus*. In Willette Frahm, M., ed., Proceedings of the Association of Reptilian and Amphibian Veterinarians, pp. 25–27. Kansas City, MO; 1998.

80. Lock, B.A., Heard, D.J., and Dennis, P. Preliminary evaluation of medetomidine/ketamine combinations for immobilization and reversal with atipamezole in three tortoise species. Bull Assoc Rept Amphib Vet; 8(4):6–9; 1998.

81. Divers, S.J. The use of propofol in reptile anesthesia. In
     Willette Frahm, M., ed., Proceedings of the Association of
     Reptilian and Amphibian Veterinarians, pp. 57–59. Tampa,
     FL; 1996.

82. Bennett, R.A., Schumacher, J., Hedjazi-Haring, K., and New-
     ell, S.M. Cardiopulmonary and anesthetic effects of propofol
     administered intra-osseously in green iguanas. J Am Vet Med
     Assoc 212:93; 1998.

83. Anderson, N.L., Wack, R.F., Burke, L., Hetherington, T., and
     Williams, J. Assessment of propofol as an anethetic agent in
     brown tree snakes, *Boiga irregularis*. In Willette Frahm, M.,
     ed., Proceedings of the Association of Reptilian and Amphib-
     ian Veterinarians, pp. 29–31. Kansas City, MO; 1998.

84. Clyde, V.C., Cardeilhac, P., and Jacobson, E. Chemical
     restraint of American alligators, *Alligator mississippiensis*,
     with atracurium or tiletamine-zolazepam. J Zoo Wildl Med
     25:525–530; 1994.

85. Mader, D.R. Reproductive surgery in the green iguana. Sem
     Avian Exotic Pet Med 5(4):214–221; 1996.

86. Divers, S.J., and Lawton, M.P.C. Personal communication;
     1998. Exotic Animal Centre, Romford, Essex, U.K.

Rodent Drug Dosages

John E. Harkness, DVM, MS, MEd

General Guidelines

Most of the general information provided in this text on drug use for other animal groups is applicable also to rodents. Some general considerations and admonitions include:

1. Although many more drugs than those listed in the table that follows these guidelines have been administered to rodents (in the U.S. Food and Drug Administration approval process, in practice, as described in formularies in reference texts, or as described on the Internet), only a small number of drugs have been shown to be efficacious and relatively safe through controlled clinical trials or long and successful use in veterinary practice. Many of those drugs, some seldom used currently, are included in the table.

2. In general practice, dosages are often based primarily on a few literature reports, empirical observations, interspecies extrapolation, and previously published, sometimes inaccurate information. The dosages given in the following table are derived from all of those sources but represent dosage ranges used frequently in rodent veterinary care. Dosages for chinchillas are in most cases in the same range as dosages for guinea pigs.

3. Virtually all drugs listed in the table are used extra-label, which necessitates a veterinarian-owner relationship, knowledge of the species and its medical care, and certain record-keeping and label requirements.

4. There have been few published, controlled studies conducted in rodents of drug pharmacokinetics, comparisons among cytochrome P450 iso-enzyme activities, protein binding, hepatic blood flow, allometric scaling, or effects of weight–body surface ratio. For all of the drugs listed in the table, the effects on dosage of gender, age, diet, health status, time of day, breeding status, species variations, microflora components, nutritional status, other drugs used, cecal mass, and aeromatic hydrocarbons from cedar and pine bedding must be considered.

5. The most common treatment considerations for sick rodents, such as fluids for hydration, food protein level (should be 16% crude protein or higher), caloric intake, and heat, are not mentioned in the table (except for vitamin C in guinea pigs). Preventive strategies include healthy stock, good sanitation, appropriately balanced diet, and proper environment. Satisfying these considerations is essential before and during drug treatment.

6. Drugs are not necessarily administered easily to rodents in a convenient volume. Pills are best delivered in suspension, intramuscular injections often cause pain and are difficult to deliver into the small limb muscles, and intravenous injections are difficult except in mice (unless one has specialized training). Subcutaneous and intraperitoneal routes are often satisfactory and are the only reasonable methods in many situations.

7. Many antimicrobials cause adverse effects in rodents, including direct toxicities of several sorts and often fatal enteropathies. Guinea pigs and hamsters, for example, can be safely given only a few antimicrobials.

8. Allometric scaling, or basing a dosage on various ana-
tomic and physiologic characteristics (e.g., smaller animals
receive higher dosages per unit weight), is described in several articles.[1,2] For one method, the following multipliers of
the guinea pig dosage are used: rat = 1.1; hamster = 1.3;
gerbil = 1.5; and mouse = 2.3. Scaling may be useful for
dosages of tetracyclines, erythromycin, diazepam, gentamicin, and carbenicillin, but it is useless for fentanyl, ketamine, chloramphenicol, and trimethoprim.

Additional Guidelines for Specific Drug Categories

Antimicrobial Agents

Antimicrobials that are used often and safely in rodents are chloramphenicol, the fluoroquinolones, the trimethoprim-sulfa combinations,
and griseofulvin. Other relatively safe drugs include gentamicin,
doxycycline, metronidazole, and some sulfa drugs. Drugs with direct,
significant toxic or neurologic effects on one or repeated doses are
gentamicin, dihydrostreptomycin, acepromazine (gerbils), procaines
(mice and guinea pigs), and amitraz.[3]

The major concern with antimicrobial use in hamsters and guinea
pigs is the delayed (3–10 days following administration) occurrence
of a usually fatal enterotoxemia with or without the sign of diarrhea.[4]
The causative agent in hamsters is usually the toxin produced by
Clostridium difficile, which is contracted from the environment by
hamsters with already altered microbial flora. Antimicrobials enter-
ing the large intestine lead to the problem.

Antimicrobial use in rodents should be neither the first nor the only
treatment, even when the diagnosis and appropriate drugs are
known.[5–7] Appropriate husbandry, alternative treatments, culture and

sensitivity, and prognosis following treatment must be considered first. Enteropathies are treated rarely with antimicrobials, but pneumonias, ocular and dental lesions, and skin diseases may respond to antimicrobial use.

Antiparasitic Agents

These agents, with the exception of amitraz and ivermectins in certain mouse strains, are usually safe. Intestinal parasite infections, such as *Giardia* and *Hymenolepus,* rarely cause clinical signs. Ectoparasitism, however, is common, and ivermectin is useful in many cases.

Preanesthetic, Anesthetic, and Analgesic Agents

A number of useful agents and dosages are included in the following table. Ketamine in various combinations with other agents and isoflurane remain the best anesthetic choices available, at least in North America. Buprenorphine is probably the most popular analgesic in rodents because of the drug's long duration of action (6–12 hours).[8] Because atropine thickens secretions in an already narrow respiratory system, glycopyrrolate is preferred as a preanesthetic.[9]

Other Drugs

Vitamin K is useful for the treatment of poisonings, ascorbic acid is essential in the guinea pig's diet, and cimetidine, cisapride, and other drugs are used occasionally for conditions related to those seen in other species.

For Further Reading

Much valuable information can be obtained from general texts or chapters on general veterinary pharmacology or on drug use in exotic animals. For some useful sources of information, see references 10–19 following the formulary table.

Drug Dosages for Rodents

ANTIMICROBIAL AGENTS

DRUG DOSE AND ROUTE	COMMENTS
Amikacin	
2–5 mg/kg *q* 8h SC, IM, or 8–16 mg/kg total per day, divided *q* 12–24h SC, IM	Aminoglycoside used occasionally for *Staphylococcus* (e.g., pododermatitis) and gram-negative infections. Animal should be hydrated well because of nephrotoxicity risk. Does not penetrate abscesses well.
Ampicillin/Amoxicillin	
Guinea pigs, 6 mg/kg *q* 8h for 5 days SC Gerbils, rats, mice, 20–100 mg/kg *q* 8h PO, SC	Used rarely in guinea pigs and hamsters because of probable induction of enterotoxemia.[20] Higher dosages lethal in guinea pigs.
Chloramphenicol palmitate	
Guinea pigs, 50 mg/kg *q* 8–12h PO Small rodents, 50–200 mg/kg *q* 8h PO	Avoid contamination of human body surface and gastrointestinal tract with chloramphenicol. This product may not be available in some areas of the United States.
Chloramphenicol succinate	
30–50 mg/kg *q* 6–12h SC, IM	Generally safe and useful in weaned and nonpregnant rodents. Inhibits microsomal enzymes. Prolongs ketamine-xylazine anesthesia in rats.

IM = intramuscularly
IP = intraperitoneally
IV = intravenously
PO = per os; orally
SC = subcutaneously

continued

117

Ciprofloxacin

7–20 mg/kg q 12h PO

Useful for gram-negative, *Staphylococcus,* and *Mycoplasma* infections. Animal should be hydrated well. Fluoroquinolones may cause defects and erosions in juvenile cartilage.

Doxycycline

2.5–5 mg/kg q 12h PO

Occasional use for mycoplasmal and bacterial pneumonias in nonpregnant murine rodents.

Enrofloxacin

2.5–20 mg/kg q 12–24h PO, SC, IM, or 50–200 mg/L water for 14 days

Used in adult animals (e.g., in rats) for mycoplasmal and gram-negative bacterial infections. Causes irritation at injection site and causes erosion of joint cartilage in young.

Erythromycin

500 mg/gal. water continuously

Useful for prevention of enteritis in colonies of hamsters.[21] Lethal at dosages higher than 500 mg/gal. drinking water. Half-life in mice is 40 minutes.

Gentamicin

2–8 mg/kg total per day, divided q 8–24h SC, IM, or 5 ml of 0.6% wt. vol. q 12h for 3 days PO

One hour half-life; oto- and nephrotoxic, more so in albinos.[22] Hydration is necessary. Lethal at 1 mg q 8h PO in hamsters. Half-life in rodents is 40–60 minutes.

Griseofulvin

15–50 mg/kg q 12h for 14–28 days PO; 1.5% in dimethyl sulfoxide for 5–7 days topically; or 300 g/ton guinea pig pellets

Treatments usually prolonged and can cause diarrhea, leukopenia, and anorexia.[23,24]

Metronidazole

Rodents generally,
10–40 mg/kg *q* 12–24h PO
or 2.5 mg/ml drinking water
for 5–14 days
Gerbils and hamsters, 7.5
mg/kg *q* 8h PO

Used for treating enteric disease or
Fusobacterium infection in rodents, including
hamsters, but not chinchillas. May erode joint
cartilage. Used for giardiasis and anaerobic
infections. Sucrose reduces aftertaste.

Neomycin

Guinea pigs, 5–30 mg/kg *q*
12–24h PO
Small rodents, 50–100 mg/kg
q 24h PO

Little efficacy noted for enteric conditions. Used
occasionally in colony situations.

Oxytetracycline

20–60 mg/kg SC, IM, or
0.25–1.0 mg/ml in drinking
water for 2 weeks

May prevent antibiotic-induced enteritis in
rodents.[25,26] Plasma levels too low to be
effective against most disease agents. Not
used with methoxyflurane. Toxic in guinea
pigs at therapeutic dosages.

Penicillin

40,000–60,000 IU/kg SC, IM

Not used in guinea pigs and hamsters because
it may cause enterotoxemia.[27] Procaine in
procaine penicillin is toxic in mice, as is
dihydrostreptomycin.[28]

Sulfadimethoxine

10–20 mg/kg *q* 12h PO or
25–50 mg/kg *q* 24h for
1–14 days PO

Used occasionally for treating bacterial
infections.

continued

Tetracycline

10–20 mg/kg *q* 8h PO; 50 mg/kg *q* 12h PO; or 400 mg/L water for 10 days

May not achieve therapeutic level in plasma when given PO.[29,30] Used in water to prevent proliferative ileitis. Half-life in mice is 1.3 hours. Toxic at 50–100 mg/kg PO. Toxic in guinea pigs at therapeutic dosages.

Trimethoprim-sulfonamide combinations

15–30 mg/kg *q* 12h PO, SC, IM

Lower dose for sulfamethoxazole combination: 5 mg/kg *q* 24h for 6 weeks PO

Useful and usually safe for bacterial infections, except in rodents with renal disease (common in rats and hamsters). Animals must be hydrated well. Dose of 33 mg/kg trimethoprim PO causes death in hamsters. Injectable product not available in the United States.

ANTIPARASITIC AGENTS

DRUG DOSE AND ROUTE	COMMENTS

Albendazole

50–100 mg/kg PO or 25 mg/kg for 3 days PO

For giardiasis. The drug is teratogenic. See fenbendazole, which is safer.

Amitraz liquid

60–250 ppm active drug in solution; 3–6 applications topically at 14-day intervals

Has been used for treating *Demodex* in rodents, but can cause death. Use sparingly on a wetted swab. Reversed by yohimbine.

Carbaryl 5% powder

Dust sparingly once or twice weekly

Overdose may be reversed by atropine. Useful against ectoparasites.

Fenbendazole

20–25 mg/kg *q* 24h for 3–5 days PO

Used to treat giardiasis and nematodiasis in small rodents.

Ivermectin

For endoparasites, 2.0 mg/kg every 7–10 days (0.008 mg/ml drinking water) PO

For ectoparasites on mice, 200 mcg/kg given twice at 10-day intervals SC or 1% ivermectin diluted 1:100 with 1:1 propylene glycol:water sprayed onto mice

For ectoparasites on guinea pigs, 300–500 mcg/kg in 2 doses repeated at 7–10 days SC

Water-soluble preparations are useful.[31–34] Generally safe for treating ecto- and endoparasites. Questionably effective against *Demodex*. C57BL mice and other strains may be especially sensitive to ivermectin.

Permethrin

Cottonball soaked in 5% active ingredient for 4–5 weeks in cage or as 0.25% dust

Useful for treating ectoparasitism in rodents.

Piperazine adipate

3–7 mg/ml drinking water for 3–10 days or 7-days-on, 7-days-off, repeat

Used occasionally for treating ectoparasitism in rodents.

Praziquantel

5–10 mg/kg PO, SC, IM; repeat in 10 days

Possible use for cestodiasis in rodents.

Sulfadimethoxine

10–20 mg/kg q 12h PO or 25–50 mg/kg q 24h for 10–14 days PO

Used for protozoal enteropathies.

continued

Thiabendazole

100–200 mg/kg PO or 0.3% in feed for 5–14 days — For treating nematodiosis. Fenbendazole is preferred for this purpose.

PREANESTHETIC AGENTS

DRUG DOSE AND ROUTE — COMMENTS

Acepromazine maleate

Guinea pigs, 0.5–1.0 mg/kg IM or 1.0–2.5 mg/kg SC
Hamsters, 5.0 mg/kg SC or 2–5 mg/kg IP — Useful adjunct with ketamine. Not for use in gerbils (causes seizures), and not for analgesia.

Atropine sulfate

Small rodents, 0.04–0.1 mg/kg SC, IM
Guinea pigs, up to 0.2 mg/kg SC — May not be effective in rats, and does thicken respiratory secretions. Dosages to 10 mg/kg in organophosphate poisoning, or to effect.

Diazepam

Rodents generally, 5–15 mg/kg SC, IM, IP
Rats and guinea pigs, 1–5 mg/kg SC, IM, IP — High injection volume. Insoluble in water; used with ketamine, which is a popular combination. Half-life in mice is 8 minutes.

Glycopyrrolate

10–20 mcg/kg IM — Give 15 minutes before anesthetic. Prevents heart rate depression in anesthetized rats.

Medetomidine

0.5 mg/kg IM — Useful for guinea pig anesthesia when combined with tiletamine-zolazepam.

Midazolam

0.3–5 mg/kg IM, IP — Water soluble and lipid soluble at body pH, and has a shorter action than does diazepam.

Tiletamine-zolazepam

3 mg/kg IM — Used for sedation before inhalant anesthesia applied. Mixture used alone may give inadequate analgesia.[35]

Xylazine

Guinea pigs, 1–3 mg/kg IM
Hamsters and mice,
5–10 mg/kg IM — Used often with ketamine, but depression of vital systems can be profound and dangerous. Often overdosed.

ANESTHETIC AGENTS

DRUG DOSE AND ROUTE — COMMENTS

Bupivacaine

0.25–0.5 mg/kg 0.25% solution q 6–8h SC or 0.5 ml 0.125% solution q 6–8h SC for 1-in. incision — Adverse reactions to overdose include seizures and cardiac dysrhythmias. Other local anesthetics may be used also.[36]

Ketamine hydrochloride

Rats and mice, 40–80 mg/kg SC, IP
Guinea pigs and chinchillas, 20–60 mg/kg IM, IP
Hamsters, 80–150 mg/kg IP
Gerbils, 40–100 mg/kg IP — Used with xylazine (2.5 mg/kg), diazepam (5 mg/kg), acepromazine (0.1–2.5 mg/kg), or medetomidine (0.25–0.5 mg/kg); drug should be given to effect and may require inhalant anesthetic also.[37,38] Ketamine causes tissue damage at injection site. Adverse effects occur if combined with detomidine.

continued

123

Pentobarbital sodium

30–40 mg/kg IP for sedation
Mice, 50–90 mg/kg (diluted)
  IP
Rats, 40–60 mg/kg IP or
  60–100 mg/kg IM
Guinea pigs, 15–40 mg/kg IP
  (20–25 mg/kg IM when
  given with 1–8 mg/kg
  diazepam)
Hamsters, 70–90 mg/kg IP
Gerbils, 36–100 mg/kg IP

This drug used in rodents causes respiratory depression, variable analgesia, slowed metabolism, and peritoneal inflammation. The drug is diluted in normal saline and given IP to effect. There is overlap of lethal and anesthetic dosages. Anethesia with single IP injection lasts 15–60 minutes.

Propofol

Mice, 12–26 ml/kg IV
Rats, 5–10 ml/kg IV or 1–2
  ml/kg IV for induction, then
  4–6 ml/kg/h to effect

Intravenous injections are not done easily in these species. Higher dosages produce around 30 minutes of anesthesia.

Thiopental

Mice, 25–50 mg/kg IV (tail vein)
Rats, 20–40 mg/kg IV

Short-acting barbiturate.

Tiletamine-zolazepam

Gerbils and hamsters,
  50–70 mg/kg IM (anesthesia);
  10–40 mg/kg IM, IP
  (sedation); 10–30 mg/kg IM
  if used with acepromazine
  (anesthesia)
Mice, 80 mg/kg IP (anesthesia)
Guinea pigs, 10–80 mg/kg IM,
  IP (sedation); combination
  of 40 mg/kg tiletamine-
  zolazepam and 0.5 mg/kg
  medetomidine or 5 mg/kg
  xylazine IM (anesthesia)

Central nervous system excitation occurs in rats and mice, but analgesia does occur at higher dosages. Central nervous system depression and poor anesthesia occur in guinea pigs.[35]

ANALGESIC AGENTS[13,36]

DRUG DOSE AND ROUTE	COMMENTS
Acetaminophen	
100–300 mg/kg q 4h PO, IP	Can be given in drinking water. Visceral and nociceptive pain require higher dosages. Acetaminophen at 50–200 mg/kg IP is equivalent to 0.2 mg/kg buprenorphine.[8]
Acetaminophen/ codeine phosphate	
1 ml elixer/100 ml drinking water	This and other over-the-counter analgesics are not used often in rodents; efficacy is
Oral solution: 120 mg/12 mg per 5 ml	uncertain.
Aspirin	
Rats and mice, 80–120 mg/kg q 4h PO or 20 mg/kg SC	Not for deep visceral or acute pain. Can be dissolved in drinking water.
Hamsters and gerbils, 300–400 mg/kg q 24h PO or 20 mg/kg SC	
Guinea pigs, 86 mg/kg PO or 270 mg/kg q 24h IP	
Buprenorphine	
Rodents generally, 2.5 mg/kg q 6–12h SC, IP	This drug's 6–12 hour effect makes it useful for analgesia in rodents.[8] Give preoperatively.
Rats, 0.1–1.0 mg/kg SC	
Guinea pigs, 0.05–0.1 mg/kg SC or 3.9 mg/kg/d in drinking water	

continued

Butorphanol tartrate

Mice, 5–10 mg/kg PO or
0.5–5.4 mg/kg *q* 4h SC
Rats, 0.04–23.3 mg/kg SC or
2.1 mg/kg PO

This drug's 2–4 hour effect provides some
analgesia.

Flunixin meglumine

2.5 mg/kg IM

Irritation when given by SC route; efficacy is
minimal in rodents.

Ibuprofen

Mice, 7.5 mg/kg PO
Rats and guinea pigs, 10–30
mg/kg *q* 4h PO

Efficacy is uncertain in rodents; drug should be
used with care.

Meperidine

Rodents, 10–20 mg/kg *q* 2–6h
SC, IM

The effect of analgesia lasts 2–3 hours or less.
Causes sedation and respiratory depression,
which can be dangerous.

Oxymorphone

Rats, 0.2–0.5 mg/kg SC
Hamsters, 0.15 mg/kg IM

These dosages have a 4-hour effect. Potent
analgesic, but little used in rodents.

Pentazocine

Mice, 1–21 mg/kg SC
Rats, 8–10 mg/kg SC

These dosages have a 3–4 hour effect. Can be
given orally.

REVERSAL AGENTS

DRUG DOSE AND ROUTE	COMMENTS

Atropine

10 mg/kg every 20 min. SC

Reversal agent for organophosphate overdose,
but may cause cardiovascular irregularities.

Doxapram

5 mg/kg IV or 10–15 mg/kg
SC, IM

Respiratory stimulant.

Nalorphine

2 mg/kg IV   Reversal agent for fentanyl overdose.

Vitamin K$_1$

1–10 mg/kg IM as needed for   For treatment of warfarin poisoning.
  4–6 days

2.5–5.0 mg/kg IM for 3–4   For treatment of brodifacoum poisoning.
  weeks

Yohimbine

0.5–1.0 mg/kg IV   For reversing xylazine and central nervous
                                system amitraz effects.

MISCELLANEOUS AGENTS

DRUG DOSE AND ROUTE	COMMENTS

Ascorbic acid

7–30 mg/kg *q* 24h SC, PO   For prevention of vitamin C deficiency (lower
                                dosage) and treatment of hypovitaminosis in
                                guinea pigs.

**Atropine 1% +
phenylephrine 10%**

1 drop topically 3–4 times   Causes mydriasis in rodents with uveal
  within 15 min.   melanin.[39]

Cimetidine

5–10 mg/kg *q* 6–12h SC, PO,   May be used to treat stress or glucocorticoid-
  IM   induced gastric ulcers.

Cisapride

0.5 mg/kg *q* 8h PO   For treatment of suspected gastric stasis
                                disorders when no blockage is present.

Dexamethasone

0.5–2.0 mg/kg PO, SC, then   Used rarely with antibiotics if inflammation itself
  decreasing dose *q* 12h for   is a problem.
  3–14 days PO, SC

continued

Dimethyl sulfoxide (DMSO)

As topical gel, 90% DMSO — For use alone or questionably with antibiotics for pododermatitis in guinea pigs and with griseofulvin for dermatophytosis.[23] Steroid may be added.

Furosemide

2–5 mg/kg *q* 12h PO, SC, IM — Occasional use for heart failure or pulmonary edema.

Oxytocin

0.1–3.0 units/kg SC, IM — For dystocia assuming fetuses cannot be removed by pulling, cervix is dilated, and uterus responds.

Prednisone

0.5–2 mg/kg SC, PO — Rarely used glucocorticoid in rodents.

Tropicamide 1%

Topical solution — Causes mydriasis except in pigmented eyes.[40]

References

1. Ings, R.M.J. Interspecies scaling and comparisons in drug development and toxicokinetics. Xenobiotica 20:1201–1231; 1990.

2. Riviere, J.E., Martin-Jimenez, T., Sundlof, S.F., and Craigmill, A.L. Interspecies allometric analysis of the comparative pharmacokinetics of 44 drugs across veterinary and laboratory species. J Vet Pharmacol Ther 20:453–463; 1997.

3. Harkness, J.E., and Wagner, J.E. The biology and medicine of rabbits and rodents. 4th ed. Baltimore, MD: Williams and Wilkins; 1995.

4. Small, J.D. Drugs used in hamsters with a review of antibiotic-associated colitis. In Hoosier, G.L., Jr., and McPherson, C.W., eds., Laboratory hamsters, pp. 179–199. Orlando, FL: Academic Press; 1987.

5. Morris, T.H. Antibiotic therapeutics in laboratory animals. Lab Anim 29:16–36; 1994.

6. Smith, D.A., and Burgmann, P.M. Formulary. In Hillyer, E.H., and Quesenberry, K.E., eds., Ferrets, rabbits, and rodents—Clinical medicine and surgery, pp. 392–403. Philadelphia: W.B. Saunders; 1996.

7. Rosenthal, K.L. Antimicrobial therapy in exotics: Vol. 20. Bacterial infections and antibiotic therapy in small mammals. Pamphlet published by Bayer Corporation, Shawnee Mission, KS; 1998.

8. Cooper, D.M., DeLong, D., and Gillett, C.S. Analgesic efficacy of acetaminophen and buprenorphine administered in the drinking water of rats. Contemp Topics 36:58–62; 1997.

9. Olson, M.E., Vizzutti, D., Morck, D.W., and Cox, A.K. The parasympatholytic effects of atropine sulfate and glycopyrrolate in rats and rabbits. Can J Vet Res 57:254-258; 1994.

10. Allen, D.G. Handbook of veterinary drugs. 2nd ed. Philadelphia: Lippincott-Raven; 1998.

11. Baker, H.J., Lindsey, J.R., and Weisbroth, S.H., eds. The laboratory rat. Vol. 2. New York: Academic Press; 1980.

12. Borchard, R.E., Barnes, C.D., and Eltherington, L.G. Drug dosage in laboratory animals—A handbook. 3rd ed. Caldwell, NJ: Telford Press; 1989.

13. Flecknell, P.A. Laboratory animal anaesthesia: A practical introduction for research workers and technicians. 2nd ed. London: Academic Press; 1996.

14. Hawk, C.T., and Leary, S.L. Formulary for laboratory animals. Ames: Iowa State University Press; 1995.

15. Hillyer, E.V., and Quesenberry, K.E. Ferrets, rabbits, and rodents: Clinical medicine and surgery. Philadelphia: W.B. Saunders; 1996.

16. Johnson-Delaney, C.A. Exotic companion medicine handbook for veterinarians. Lake Worth, FL: Wingers Publishing; 1996.

17. Laber-Laird, K., Flecknell, P., and Swindle, M.M. Handbook of rabbit and rodent medicine. New York: Elsevier; 1995.

18. Marx, K.L., and Roston, M.A. The exotic animal drug compendium. Trenton, NJ: Veterinary Learning Systems; 1996.

19. Van Hoosier, G.L., Jr., and McPherson, C.W., eds. Laboratory hamsters. Orlando, FL: Academic Press; 1987.

20. Young, J.D., Hurst, W.J., White, J.W., and Lang, C.M. An evaluation of ampicillin pharmacokinetics and toxicity in guinea pigs. Lab Anim Sci 37:652–656; 1987.

21. LaRegina, M., Fales, W.H., and Wagner, J.E. Effects of antibiotic treatment on the occurrence of experimentally induced proliferative ileitis of hamsters. Lab Anim Sci 30:38–41; 1980.

22. Conlee, J.W., Gill, S.S., McCandless, P.T., and Creel, D.J. Differential susceptibility to gentamicin ototoxicity between albino and pigmented guinea pigs. Hearing Res 41:43–52; 1989.

23. Post, K., and Saunders, J.R. Topical treatment of experimental ringworm in guinea pigs with griseofulvin in dimethylsulfoxide. Can Vet J 20:45–48; 1979.

24. Valiant, M.E., and Frost, B.M. An experimental model for evaluation of antifungal agents in a *Trichophyton mentagrophytes* infection of guinea pigs. Chemotherapy 30:54–60; 1984.

25. Baxter, P., and McKellar, Q. Plasma and lung concentrations of oxytetracycline after its intramuscular administration in rats. Lab Anim Sci 45:107–109; 1995.

26. Curl, J.L., Curl, J.S., and Harrison, J.K. Pharmacokinetics of long acting oxytetracycline in the laboratory rat. Lab Anim Sci 38:430–434; 1988.

27. Lowe, B.R., Fox, J.G., and Bartlett, J.G. *Clostridium difficile*–associated cecitis in guinea pigs exposed to penicillin. Am J Vet Res 41:1277–1279; 1980.

28. Galloway, J.H. Antibiotic toxicity in white mice. Lab Anim Care 18:421–425; 1968.

29. Porter, W.P., Bitar, Y.S., Strandberg, J.D., and Charache, P.C. Absence of therapeutic blood concentrations of tetracycline in rats after administration in drinking water. Lab Anim Sci 35:71–75; 1985.

30. McNeil, P.E., Al-Mashat, R.R., Bradley, R.A., and Payne, A.P. Control of an outbreak of wet tail in a closed colony of hamsters (*Mesocricetus auratus*). Vet Rec 119:272–273; 1986.

31. Baumans, V., Haverracer, R., Van Herck, H., and Rooymans, T.P. The effectiveness of Ivomec and Neguvon in the control of murine mites. Lab Anim 22:243–245; 1988.

131

32. Flynn, B.M., Brown, P.A., Eckstein, J.M., and Strong, D. Treatment of *Syphacia obvelata* in mice using ivermectin. Lab Anim Sci 39:461–463; 1989.

33. Levee, E.M., Klinger, M.M., Kaiser, C.C., and Serrano, L.J. A practical delivery method for oral administration of ivermectin to large colonies of rodents. Contemp Topics 33:68–70; 1994.

34. McKellar, Q.A., Midgley, D.M., Galbraith, E.A., Scott, E.W., and Bradley, A. Clinical and pharmacological properties of ivermectin in rabbits and guinea pigs. Vet Rec 130:71–73; 1992.

35. Buchanan, K.C., Burge, R.R., and Ruble, G.R. Evaluation of injectable anesthetics for major surgical procedures in guinea pigs. Contemp Topics 37:58–63; 1998.

36. Dawson, D.L., and Scott-Conner, C. Adjunctive use of local anesthetic infiltration during guinea pig laparotomy. Lab Animal 17:35–36; 1988.

37. Spikes, S.E., Hoogstraten-Miller, S.L., and Miller, G.F. Comparison of five anesthetic agents administered intraperitoneally in the laboratory rat. Contemp Topics 35:53–56; 1996.

38. Frisk, C.S., Herman, M.D., and Senta, K.E. Guinea pig anesthesia using various combinations and concentrations of ketamine, xylazine, and/or acepromazine. Lab Anim Sci 32:434; 1982.

39. Liles, J.H., and Flecknell, P.A. The use of non-steroidal anti-inflammatory drugs for the relief of pain in laboratory rodents and rabbits. Lab Anim 26:241–255; 1992.

40. Belhorn, R.W. Laboratory animal ophthalmology. In Gelatt, K.N., ed., Veterinary ophthalmology, pp. 656–679. Philadelphia: Lea & Febiger; 1991.